JESSICA SWALE

Jessica Swale is an award-winning writer and director. She trained at Central School of Speech and Drama and the University of Exeter.

Her plays include *Nell Gwynn*, which premiered at Shakespeare's Globe before transferring to the West End, and won the 2016 Oliver Award for Best New Comedy, and *Blue Stockings*, which won her a nomination for Most Promising Playwright in the Evening Standard Awards 2013. She is now writing the screenplay, and an original film, *Summerland*, after winning a JJ Screenwriting Bursary from BAFTA.

Jessica is Artistic Director of Red Handed Theatre Company, which is dedicated to creating new work and rediscovering forgotten plays. Recent productions include *The Rivals* starring Celia Imrie, the London premiere of *Palace of the End* by Judith Thompson, and the first major revival of Hannah Cowley's *The Belle's Stratagem*, which won her a nomination for Best Director at the Evening Standard Awards.

Other direction includes *Bedlam* (Shakespeare's Globe); *Sleuth* (Watermill); *Fallen Angels* (Salisbury Playhouse); *Winter* (TNL, Canada); *The Busy Body*, *Someone to Watch Over Me* (Southwark), *The School for Scandal* (Park Theatre); and productions at RADA and LAMDA. Jessica was Max Stafford-Clark's Associate Director at Out of Joint from 2007–2010.

Jessica is an associate artist with Youth Bridge Global, an international NGO which uses theatre as a tool for promoting social change in war-torn and developing nations. As such, she has lived in the Marshall Islands and in Bosnia and Herzegovina, directing Shakespeare productions including *The Comedy of Errors*, *Much Ado About Nothing*, *Twelfth Night* and *The Tempest*.

She has written two other titles in the *Drama Games* series: *for Classrooms and Workshops*, and *for Rehearsals*.

drama games

A series of books for teachers, workshop leaders, directors and actors in need of new and dynamic activities when working in education, workshop or rehearsal.

*The publisher welcomes suggestions
for further titles in the series.*

Jessica Swale

drama games

FOR DEVISING

Foreword by Mike Leigh

NICK HERN BOOKS
London
www.nickhernbooks.co.uk

A Nick Hern Book

DRAMA GAMES FOR DEVISING

First published in Great Britain in 2012
by Nick Hern Books Limited
The Glasshouse, 49a Goldhawk Road,
London W12 8QP

Reprinted 2012, 2014, 2015, 2016, 2017, 2018

Cover designed by www.energydesignstudio.com
Typeset by Nick Hern Books, London
Printed and bound in Great Britain by
Ashford Colour Press, Gosport, Hampshire

A CIP catalogue record for this book
is available from the British Library

ISBN   978 1 84842 037 3

MIX
Paper from
responsible sources
FSC® C011748

For Jill and Robin Swale
and Muriel Norman,
who taught me that playing games
can be the best form of education

'No man is an island, entire of itself;
every man is a piece of the continent,
a part of the main.'

John Donne

'I personally would like to bring a tortoise onto
the stage, turn it into a racehorse, then into a hat,
a song, a dragon and a fountain of water. One can
dare anything in the theatre and it's the place
where one dares the least.'

Eugène Ionesco

FOREWORD

Far from being an anomaly invented in the Swinging Sixties, so-called 'devised theatre' is as old as society itself. Millennia before the birth of the formal literary 'script', we can be sure that folk got on their feet and made things up. Long nights round ancient campfires would be filled by endlessly inventive home-made entertainments. Singers of songs, tellers of stories and jokes, and groups of performers acting out yarns they had cooked up collaboratively, sometimes led by prehistoric versions of directors, often not, would light up the darkness.

It is inconceivable that the theatrical companies of Ancient Greece and Rome put together their productions of Sophocles and Plautus without group experiment and improvisation, and we know from the Folios that much extemporisation and collaborative creativity took place in Shakespeare's theatre.

From *Commedia dell'Arte* to Victorian burlesque, from music hall and pantomime to the silent cinema of Keaton, Chaplin, Griffiths, Feuillade, von Stroheim et al., from the agit-prop theatre of the 1930s to the Goons and Pythons, making it up is as natural as laughing and crying.

A play in performance is an organic, visceral, three-dimensional thing. It isn't, by definition, the reading out of a text. So it is entirely logical to create live theatre directly. The currency, the medium, is people: physical action in time and space – not merely words on a page.

And the world is out there, waiting for us to depict it, in all its joy and pain.

Just make up a play. It's easy. Or is it? Well, it is, once you get the ball rolling. But kicking off can often be difficult. For some, it's just the question of having an idea, and getting on with it. But for others, especially when we remember that we are talking about group creativity, ways are needed to stimulate ideas – to release the collective imagination.

And that is the unique value of this highly original and massively useful book. With impressive thoroughness, Jessica Swale has assembled a remarkable compendium of games and exercises.

Everything here qualifies as a lively starting point for rich invention. But, as an experienced and talented director, Jessica knows that the building of a solid ensemble is as important as the play itself, so much of what you will find in these pages will be equally useful for that purpose alone.

This book is a great achievement, and you will have much fun with it. Happy play-making!

Mike Leigh

CONTENTS

Index of Games

INTRODUCTION

If you take the time to stop by a park or a playground anywhere in the world, you will observe the same phenomenon. Groups of youngsters making believe. Darting about as aliens, swaggering around on a pirate ship or leaping over logs as if they are horses, children love to make things up. There is a creative spirit deep-rooted in the human psyche, which yearns for just this kind of spontaneous fun. Yet somehow, as we 'grow up', the increasing demands on us to plan and prepare not only limit our opportunities for spontaneity, but reinforce a belief that to ad-lib or behave impulsively is less worthwhile.

Perhaps, in some walks of life, this is the case. But theatre is a live performance art and relies on a sense of immediacy and imaginative freedom, which is born out of extemporisation. The children in the park were not recreating stories they had been told. They were making things up, on the spot. They were devising. The joy of make-believe is its lack of constraints; a story that begins on a pirate ship might equally as well end on the moon as it might in the discovery of treasure.

Children find endless amusement in the act of improvisation, so it makes sense that if we strive to create entertaining theatre, we should follow suit. There is something profoundly satisfying about creating a story from scratch, and often plays developed within an inventive and supportive environment reflect this, to their benefit.

This book explores the devising process and looks at how to foster imaginative freedom in a rehearsal room, in order to create work that is organic, original and dynamic.

What is Devised Theatre?

Devised theatre is created during the rehearsal process, as opposed to a staged version of an extant script. In a 'conventional' rehearsal process, while the director and actors have the liberty to play with interpretation, ultimately their aim is to deliver a faithful version of the text.

In contrast, on day one of a devising project, the participants jump into the abyss of the unknown. They may have starting points in mind – a text, an object, music, a space, a concept or issue – but at this stage no one will have an idea of what the final production will be like. Those factors which we imagine to be the building blocks of a play – plot, characters, structure, style, form – are all yet to be decided. Unsurprisingly, this element of risk can be daunting. However, it also engenders an immense sense of fun and freedom, the opportunity to try things out, to experiment and to play.

Devised theatre can be fresh, original, captivating and thrilling. Whilst the prospect of devising might initially provoke panic – 'What do you mean, we have to create a play from scratch?!' – it is, I think, often the most exciting way of working. There's the palpable danger, the thrill of the unknown, the excitement of the adventure, and the satisfaction of creating something entirely original. Actors and students learn invaluable skills during the devising process. Indeed, some of the most successful productions in the contemporary canon are devised, or use devising techniques in their development. Complicite's playful devising strategies are visible in their productions; they work as an ensemble under the auspices of director Simon McBurney, experimenting with visual media, object manipulation, text and narrative to create theatrically innovative work, like *A Disappearing Number* and *Shunkin*. Katie Mitchell uses collaborative devising techniques to create new interpretations of classic texts like Virginia Woolf's *Waves*. Similarly, Punchdrunk use ensemble improvisation techniques to arrive at their celebrated interactive, immersive style of performance, which has be seen in works like *The Masque of the Red Death* and *Faust*.

Devising is an opportunity to stretch your creative legs, to spread your artistic wings and to explore the act of making theatre. We should relish it and enjoy it. This book outlines games and exercises that can be used to devise your own theatre, and provides the tools to start doing just that.

Devising and the Question of Collaboration

The terms 'devised' and 'collaborative' theatre are often bandied about together or used interchangeably. They are worth unpicking in order to plan your devising process. A principal difference between devising and working conventionally on a script is the potential for collaborative authorship in the former, as opposed to the single authorial voice of the latter. Devising companies work together to generate material. This does not necessarily mean that the roles of director or playwright become obsolete; there are a variety of devising methods. A director might provide the stimulus material. They might plan creative exercises for rehearsals or may well join in as an equal participant in the initial stages of creation, stepping out to 'direct' the piece in the later stages of rehearsal.

Likewise, a writer might be brought in to shape the work or to advise on the story. They may even create a full text which draws together the various elements of the initial process. In short, there are no rules as to how collaborative a devising process must be. The goal is simply to make use of the pool of creative skills available; many heads are better than one. But how does this work, and is there a danger of too many cooks?

Text Creation in Collaboration:
Max Stafford-Clark

Many mainstream theatres are wary of devised work. Many like the concept, but would rather accept plays that use devising strategies in rehearsals but then hand over to a playwright, rather than collectively authored pieces. Naturally, there is a greater element of risk in programming something that does not yet exist; if it cannot be read, it is more difficult to assess its potential. Both fully collaborative and writer-led processes use elements of devising in their rehearsals, but the latter adheres to a more conventional rehearsal model after the writer has penned the text, resulting in a work which the playwright ultimately claims authorship of.

The celebrated work commissioned and directed by Max Stafford-Clark at the Royal Court Theatre, with Joint Stock, and subsequently with Out of Joint Theatre Company, is evidence of the success of a workshop-based method of text creation. Actors are invited to collaborate with him and the playwright, over a period of usually four weeks, in order to develop initial ideas, scenarios and questions. The aim is to inspire the writer.

Stafford-Clark's workshops are highly collaborative. Each individual's contribution is valued. Actors are encouraged to pursue improvisations in new directions, using their own creativity to develop the work. Stafford-Clark works with the playwright to find shared points of interest and then runs a series of exercises to delve into the material. This often includes interviewing individuals, undertaking primary research, using improvisations and games to form scenes and raw material – the sort of games that you can find in this book. If the play is to be a verbatim text (one created using the words of interviewees, such as *Talking to Terrorists* by Robin Soans or *The Permanent Way* by David Hare), the writer, director and actors spend time meeting and recording interviews with relevant people. At this point in the process the writer may only have a vague idea of the play, perhaps some of the characters and an outline of a story, but the work created in the rehearsal room can often lead somewhere quite different – somewhere surprising. Stafford-Clark warns that setting out to create verbatim theatre with a strong agenda or message is deadly. Engaging work derives from questions, not answers. Rather than making work to share what you already know or believe, it is far more interesting to use the process as a means of exploration.

After this initial playful period, the baton is then passed to the playwright, who is given time to develop a full script inspired by the workshop. They are completely free to use or discard the workshop material as they wish. Sometimes scenes arrived at in the workshop are replicated almost identically in the final text. Sometimes, though, it is simply questions which arise in the devising period that inspire the playwright to develop something quite original, and has no direct resemblance to the content of the workshop. Stafford-Clark has often used the mantra 'the writer is king'. Whilst he stays in close contact with the playwright over this 'writing period', by giving the writer creative space, he ensures they feel ownership of the final text.

When the play is finished, the actors are reassembled to rehearse the new play. Over the course of four or five weeks in rehearsal, he uses 'actioning' and Stanislavskian techniques, as one might with a classical text, to create a production that honours the text completely.

Stafford-Clark has used this collaborative method to create some of the most seminal works of the last forty years, including Timberlake Wertenbaker's *Our Country's Good*, David Hare's *The Permanent Way*, Howard Brenton's *Epsom Downs* and Caryl Churchill's *Serious Money*, to name a few. By pioneering this workshop method, Stafford-Clark made major innovations in British theatre and brought elements of devising into the mainstream.

A Return to the Commune: Shunt

In contrast with Out of Joint, some companies work as a creative collective throughout the rehearsal process. Working as an ensemble, they construct work without hierarchy and sometimes without a director. Shunt, for example, is a theatre collective of ten artists who create theatre 'events', which assault the senses and fascinate their audiences. They work strictly as a collective, their programmes stating 'devised by the company' rather than breaking down the creative roles.

Shunt focuses on creating large-scale interactive environments in unique spaces (their current home is the vaults under London Bridge train station). The productions are highly visual, often not following a linear narrative but creating a more abstract, sensory experience using sound, action and text. Something about the multiplicity of the work, the experiential and multilayered elements of performance, reflects the way it was created: by a group of people who each have their own ideas and interests. They work together to create the work, taking it in turns to throw ideas in, playing games and experimenting with sequences, stories and themes. Their recent work includes *Tropicana*, *Amato Saltone* and *Money*; work that has placed them firmly in the public eye.

Mischa Twitchin is one of Shunt's ten core artists. He explains that the company consciously rebel against the idea of director as an auteur, or the idea of 'the theatre' as an institution. He also explains that working as a group means negotiation is essential:

'Collaboration is the excitement between people who share a vision. Within this, any member of the team at any one moment has to make compromises. It is vital, for that reason, that we all make our own work outside Shunt to satisfy our own creative urges. The beauty of collaboration is that the work is incomparably richer than anything you could create on your own.'

So is this the ultimate in collaborative work; is it the theatrical equivalent of a Communist collective? Not entirely. The ten members of Shunt each have different skill-specific responsibilities. Twitchin is primarily a lighting designer, others are directors, designers, performers. Does the presence of a director mean that one person takes a greater level of control? Twitchin explains that inevitably decisions have to be made in order to create an event; to work without any kind of leadership would be impractical, but the collaborative nature of rehearsals mean they avoid the sense of segmented roles and 'limited relationships' which Shunt associate with traditional rehearsals:

'The benefit of a large group is that there is always a lot going on. Like any process, there's more of an impact if the director is asleep than one of the performers. These roles, like "director", exist because they have a function. But in our rehearsals we all work together. Work progresses through improvisations that are based on a theme, action or relationship that we are all interested in. Everyone contributes, we all watch to see where it is going.'

In rehearsals, Shunt use improvisation games to develop ideas. They all muck in, bringing their suggestions for themes, ideas, characters and plot. This way they generate a wealth of material, which they experiment with freely before they begin to edit it in preparation for performance. Everyone has a say. Twitchin believes that working as a collective rather than defining roles avoids the syndrome of people saying, 'That's not my job', which, he suggests, is a 'creative shutdown':

'Our process mitigates the sense of a traditional division of labour, the hierarchical system reflective of an institution rather than a process.'

Ultimately, he suggests, through empowering everyone to contribute, the work produced is richer. But isn't there an argument that designating someone (a director) as the final decision-maker is both efficient and beneficial in terms of clarity?

Perhaps this depends on the nature of the piece. Shunt's work is multilayered, fragmented, postmodern. In a more conventional, linear style of storytelling, a directorial perspective might be more valuable. Film provides a clear case for this; it is the medium that gives the director most artistic control. Film directors carefully select exactly what they want the audience to see – and filter it, pinpointing our focus. But does this mean that devising and collaboration are redundant? Absolutely not.

Starting with a Blank Page: Mike Leigh

Mike Leigh is one of Britain's most celebrated film and theatre writer-directors. His work is candid, real, detailed and innovative, and is exemplary in terms of clear storytelling. Yet he uses collaborative techniques throughout his process in order to build the work from scratch. Unlike Shunt, his devising techniques are used to create linear stories.

Leigh creates work from scratch through the rehearsal process. Whilst some devising companies begin with an objective to investigate a specific subject matter, Leigh explains that his starting point is often vague, and certainly is not oriented towards a predetermined destination. On the first day of his process there is often a question, a sense, an interest, but never a narrative, or even set of characters. Leigh uses a series of procedures to collaborate with actors in order to create characters and their worlds:

'People always ask me, do I know what I am going to do? The answer is yes and no. Sometimes it is very vague, sometimes no more than a feeling – Happy Go Lucky began with no more than a feeling, a sense of something. There's always something to evolve. The film I am making at the moment [Another Year] I had no idea about. The structure of the film came out of the dramatic need to solve the question of "How often do you need to see somebody?", justifying how often you could see somebody.'

But when the world is your oyster, where do you start? Leigh warns against the dangers of trying too hard to create 'art', proposing instead that devisers follow their gut instincts and find sources in the world around them, in their everyday experiences:

'As soon as you look out anywhere, you will find subject matter… The minute you look out there and stop thinking about "the art, the art" then it is actually interesting. Anything can be dramatised – any combination of characters – that is the startling thing, so in a way it is all common sense. The minute anyone's got any notion of what they want to look at, once they are onto something that may well lead to "something" – the content gives you all the answers… It is about using the tool called rehearsal, as opposed to secondary tools like word processors or pens. You can make things up. That's what theatre was, long before anyone wrote anything down… Access the world, tell stories about what you see.'

Leigh's plays and films often starkly explore the grimmer realities of life. His work is naturalistic, aiming to present a believable picture of real life. By working with the actors to draw characters from the landscape around them, from their own experiences, he ensures that the audience will recognise what they see and therefore engage with it on a personal level. In order to create characters, Leigh works with each actor individually:

'So I will say to you as an actor, "Think of everyone that you can, that you have ever met, who is female (or male) and within a range of X years of your age…" The record is held by Sally Hawkins [playing the lead character in Happy-Go-Lucky], who hit the two hundred and something mark… I spend a massive amount of time with each actor. To an extent, talking with someone about lots of people, on lots of levels, we're chewing the fat and building a relationship and talking about all sorts of things. What I am doing is listening and thinking, "This could be a possible source, no, yes, no, not that person but someone else" – it's a creative thing and it is freewheeling. Eventually a choice has to be made which we will use as a source. It is only a source, a jumping-off point. The character we end up with will never be a literal representation of that person.'

Leigh chooses a person, or several, from the actor's list. He explains his role as the decision-maker:

'I choose. It has to be said because that is the reality, as eventually it is about coherent storytelling. The actors do the acting. That isn't to say they don't have masses of input – because they do.'

The next stage is to physicalise the person. Samuel Beckett's mantra 'Less is more' is all-important here; Leigh encourages the actors not to attempt to be dramatic or comic, rather to be the person in real time, utterly naturalistically. This is essential to the realism at the core of his work. There are two methods used to find the physical life of the character:

'The purest way is saying, "Right… do him or her in a room with no one else there, you don't have to talk, just go into character and be the person, and stay in character until I tell you." Alternatively, the more sophisticated way is to say, "Walk around, you can be wherever you like, just be fluid, just get the feel of the person."'

If Leigh has chosen multiple people as sources rather than one, he will split the room into areas. Each source person is allocated an area of the rehearsal room. The actor must then walk around, becoming each source person according to the area they are in. Leigh then encourages the actor to move into the areas where these people merge, where the actor will create a hybrid, Person X, who exists somewhere in the middle. Thus a new character is formed.

This is the first stage of Leigh's method. Then he works with the actor to create a fuller picture of the character. They list all the details that the actor knows about the source person (or people): how old they are, where they went to school, whether they have siblings, and so on. Leigh and the actor then fill in the gaps imaginatively, making up the unknown information. Of course, if the character is a hybrid of several, the inventive work is in selecting which elements of the character stem from which source, and in melding them into one being. A great deal of the imaginative work is in questioning the known information, editing it to create a new person. X didn't go to university, but what if she had? Who would she be then? This is the stage at which, whilst plenty of the ideas come from the actor, Leigh is very much in his element as the director, the information filter. Whilst working with each actor individually, he is also painting a much bigger picture:

'My role as writer-director is to be on the go right from the beginning… It is quite easy to work with an actor and arrive at a character, but unless the decisions are motivated by some sense of how they relate to other characters, some scheme, unless there's some independent storytelling on the go, then it is completely random and arbitrary. You need to arrive at the point where you are going to convert all of this raw material into something which is distilled and written and structured. So I am cooking up a character with each actor but I am also conducting a "writerly" investigation into the subject and story.'

Leigh acts as an omnipotent author throughout, encouraging contributions from the actors, but holding the reins and shaping the work into one cohesive whole. His working method varies starkly from the ensemble process that Shunt employs, or the writer-led focus that Stafford-Clark favours. All three use devising, but within very different methodologies.

Choosing a Method

We can see from these three contrasting methods that devising can be a useful tool across many styles of theatre-making. Whilst these case studies differ in their allocation of roles and responsibilities within the creative process, essentially all three share in one philosophy: the virtue of collaboration. As John Donne said, 'No man is an island'; they believe that creativity benefits from a multiplicity of voices and perspectives.

Let us consider these two terms again: devising and collaboration. Devised theatre simply means that which is created during the rehearsal process. Collaborative theatre is work developed through acts of teamwork. So are they one and the same?

Not entirely. Many companies place collaboration at the centre of their philosophy: Filter, Kneehigh and Complicite, for example. Some actively rebel against the notion of an auteur. Improbable's Phelim McDermott claimed one of the greatest achievements of their success *Shockheaded Peter* was the fact that it went to the West End 'and you can't really say who wrote it; that in itself is a strong social statement.'

Collaboration, however, does not necessarily mean abandoning traditional roles. Kneehigh's Artistic Director Emma Rice describes how their devising method relies on working as individuals within a team:

'Months before rehearsals begin, I start work with the creative team. We gaze at books and films, sketch and begin to form a concept, an environment in which the story can live, in which the actors can play. We exchange music. Writers go away and write collections of poems or lyrics or ideas. It is this fertile palette of words, music and design that we bring to the rehearsal room. Kneehigh is a team. The shared imagination is greater than any individual's, so we begin the rehearsal process by returning to the story. We tell it to each other, scribble thoughts on huge pieces of paper, relate it to our own experience. We create characters. The design is developed with ideas coming from the devising team. The writers are in rehearsal. They watch and inspire, feeding in their poetry, their lyrics. They respond to improvisation and then craft scenes and characters alongside the actors. Layer upon layer, the world is created, the story released. If you stay true to the fundamental relationship between yourself, your team and the subject matter, the piece will take on a life of its own.'

It is quite possible to use elements of devising to create work within a conventionally structured process. The earliest devised play to become a commercial hit was probably *Oh! What a Lovely War* in 1963, devised by Joan Littlewood and her Theatre Workshop. Littlewood was a pioneer, involving her actors fully in the creation of the material, yet she maintained the role of director, initiating and shaping the work. Essentially, plays need narrative, focus and structure; even the most abstract work needs careful planning and a consideration of the audience's perspective.

Your choice of working method should reflect the type of work you want to make. Shunt work as an ensemble because they aim to create experiential, multiauthored, layered performances. Mike Leigh conducts an authorial investigation, using devising to generate material, which he then filters to create plays and films inspired very much by observed reality. Max Stafford-Clark uses exercises with his actors to assemble a rich tapestry of research, characters and stories, which he then hands to the writer, who filters it through their own personal interests and perspective. Each results in a different style of work, whilst taking advantage of the opportunity to draw from the team. In these cases, an array of different cooks might, in fact, improve the broth.

Starting Work

The joy of devising is the absolute creative freedom engendered when you can start anywhere you like. It's an adventure. Who knows where you will end up? Whilst it is fun to play, the best devised theatre often has two key traits in common.

Firstly, a sense of truthfulness and integrity. Mike Leigh warns about the dangers of setting out to create 'art'; an objective which often leads to rather pretentious and self-indulgent creations. Remember that drama is a reflection of life. Regardless of whether the content of the piece is realistic, human emotions need to be presented truthfully in order for us to engage. Disney films are hardly believable – peopled with dancing animals, princes and princesses, wicked witches and poisoned apples – but they deal with real dilemmas, and in fact the actors who voice the characters are experts in absolute believability. So whether you are creating an all-singing, all-dancing musical set on Pluto, or a kitchen-sink-style drama, your characters need to engage with humanity and emotion in order for us to care about them. Use your own experiences to shape your characters. Consider which plays, films or books have stirred you the most, and why that is, then feed this into your work.

The second trait of good devised theatre is clear storytelling that relies on establishing a set of rules and experimenting within them. Be selective with your material; this will allow you to explore it in much more depth. For example, you might well create richer work if you choose to devise a piece about suffragettes in London than if you attempted to create a play about women in general. Limit yourself, set parameters, make decisions and don't be scared to discard ideas if they don't work.

Planning Your Rehearsal Process

Anyone training at drama school or devising a piece for a school exam will no doubt be familiar with the feeling of dread as the yawning chasm of rehearsal time opens up in front of you, unplanned and empty. Those intimidating words 'performance' or 'opening night' are scrawled a few weeks hence in the diary, and the dread intensifies as the 'Big Day' looms closer. So how do you plan a devising process well?

I spent many hours as a student improvising frantically in rehearsal, hoping that divine inspiration would just arrive at some moment. Over time it became obvious that structure is vital. In a conventional script-based process, directors plan carefully to ensure the actors are ready for performance. Rehearsals may begin with an initial exploration of the text, a read-through and basic character work, followed by rough sketching-out of the scenes (walking through the scene, trying ideas out), research, blocking (planning moves), then preparation for performance (working with props, costumes, set, etc.).

It is equally important to plan devising rehearsals carefully, to ensure that the actors are well prepared. Even if there are improvisational elements in the play, decisions must still be made. Everyone needs to be absolutely sure of the rules of performance, their roles and the narrative they are trying to deliver.

By carefully planning your process you can ensure you have adequate time to experiment, to develop ideas and to structure the work so that it is both detailed and engaging. All too often we lose sight of the importance of an audience's understanding. We assume that, because we know what we are trying to say and we have witnessed the genesis of the piece, those watching will automatically 'get it' too. We forget that they have not been present for the evolution of each idea. The audience only have what they witness in performance to inform their understanding.

There are several easy traps to fall into. Often actors become so carried away with their own process that they forget their audience entirely, taking great enjoyment in their work but leaving the audience confused and frustrated. Equally dangerous is the opposite problem: some companies are so concerned about clarity that they rush decisions, leaving themselves no room to play and experiment. This can result in work which makes perfect sense but which is theatrically rather dull and pedestrian. So how do we avoid these pitfalls?

The Five Stages of Devising

There is no sure-fire recipe for success when it comes to devising. The following process is merely a suggestion, a starting point. It is a method I have developed in my own work; I find it useful but it is by no means meant to be definitive. For me, the key to successful devising is decision-making: set yourself parameters; plan ahead; do not be scared to experiment, but ensure you allow sufficient time to work on detail.

Devising should be a constant process of expansion and contraction – generating a wealth of ideas and then rejecting some; creating scenes and then revising them; developing a narrative and then streamlining it. The following five-stage process encourages you to be as imaginative and playful as possible within a carefully structured timetable.

Stage One: Preparation

In which we prepare to jump off the edge

In the first phase there are few rules, the focus is on having fun. The aim is to get to know each other, to find a common language, share skills and to warm up the body and mind ready for work.

Stage Two: Generation

In which we create an array of starting points and ideas

In the second phase we begin to generate material. We use playful techniques to initiate ideas and to generate a wealth of creative building blocks. The focus is on imagining, improvising and being open to exploring a range of stimuli before moving into the realms of decision-making. We cultivate a plethora of ideas and try them all out.

Stage Three: Exploration

In which we develop and expand our ideas

In the third phase we begin selecting and developing key ideas. We pick the most inspiring concepts from the second stage and then investigate them further. It is still a generative phase, but we begin to set parameters, pinning down basic elements of narrative, characters and scenes. By the end of this phase we should have a strong idea of the shape and themes of the piece, allowing us to move on to explore detail in the next phase.

Stage Four: Distillation

In which we selectively develop and hone our ideas – and watch the play start to emerge

Having created an outline in the third stage, at the fourth stage we now fill in the gaps, edit and reassess. We experiment with structure, consider the dynamics and flesh out characters and their relationships. We also work on shape, tension and the narrative arc until we have a piece that is almost ready for performance.

Stage Five: Presentation

In which we move from the rehearsal room to the wings

The fifth and final stage involves performance preparation. At this stage, the more conventional elements of rehearsal come into play. Key elements of performance technique – vocal projection, accent, character detail, staging, blocking and ensemble skills – become essential. The audience now becomes the focus. We concentrate on giving an energetic, honed and engaging performance, and then we begin!

How to Use This Process

This five-stage process could be used to structure your entire rehearsal period, with a given number of rehearsals allocated to each of the stages. However, if you are investigating multiple starting points, you could apply this five-stage process to each individual strand, thereby repeating it several times over the course of rehearsals. Let us look at an example.

I recently worked with two groups of drama-school students, who were tasked with devising an original piece of theatre over five weeks. Their stimulus was local myths and legends. I offered both groups the five-stage process as a means of structuring their work and asked them to apply it as they saw fit.

One group constructed a play exploring the theme of capture, which involved telling five sea myths in contrasting ways. They used the five-stage process to develop each myth separately, each time working through stages one to five, before moving on to the next story. They then used the whole process again to decide how to put the piece together. After playing some initial games (**Stage One: Preparation**), they began improvising playfully around the mythical characters (**Stage Two: Generation**). Next they selected their favourite tales and explored those in greater depth (**Stage Three: Exploration**). They considered the myths in detail and explored different performative languages in which to tell them: some told with words, others to music, others using stage combat to add dynamism and excitement, giving their piece texture and contrasts. However, as is often the case, they had then developed such a wealth of material that it became vital to edit drastically, cutting unnecessary material and paying more attention to the shape of the piece as a whole. They needed to link each as yet unconnected story. They did so by choosing a setting – a ship – and introducing each new myth as the sailors got increasingly drunk and began telling tales. They edited their narrative arc (**Stage Four: Distillation**), finding a way to shift cleverly from the world of the ship to the myths themselves. They then rehearsed with full costume and technical aspects in preparation for the performance (**Stage Five: Presentation**).

The other group took a different approach, as they were eager to focus on one story. They divided their rehearsal schedule into five parts, rigidly following the five-stage process, allocating a week per stage, in order to allow themselves enough time to develop an original yet detailed performance. In the initial weeks they brought in research about local buildings and hauntings, focusing on a newspaper article about an abandoned hospital nearby. Over the next few weeks they worked collaboratively to create characters and plot, before scripting their piece, choreographing sequences and working on performance. Their final piece was an abstract tale about a girl who has hallucinatory experiences after partying at an illegal rave in a disused hospital.

Both groups created fascinating work, yet planned their rehearsal processes in very different ways. There is clearly no 'correct' method for devising, as with any creative process. However, one cannot deny the value of planning, the benefits of experimenting and the importance of allowing yourself time to edit and to develop detail. By adhering to these basic principles you can avoid the dangers of creating either nonsensical chaos which leaves an audience frustrated, or worse, creating bland, safe theatre which encourages the most deathly audience response of all: complete indifference.

How to Use This Book

This book is set out in five chapters which correspond to these five stages of the devising process. Each contains a range of exercises which can use to help plan your rehearsals, or, if you are more like me, which you might just dip into and use when the time is right. Each exercise is set out in simple terms, listing the aims, the skills developed, and information about the number of players and any equipment required. There are also suggestions for variations and extensions for many of the games. Feel free to experiment; the rules are only guidelines. Some won't work for your process; others, I hope, you will return to again and again. Most exercises you can adapt to suit your actors, their interests and skills, and the themes or form of your piece. Break the rules, adapt the games, relish the opportunity to make them your own. It is always more fun that way.

The games are intended to provide an array of tools to help you make work from scratch. It's important to note, of course, that the creation of a fully fledged, performable play is no mean feat. Most theatre companies allocate four weeks of full-time rehearsal to work on a conventional script. And those weeks will be crammed with activity: exploration of the world of the play, research, character exercises, physical and vocal work, analysis of the text, development of an interpretation – and that's all before the play is even 'put on its feet' and staged.

If the company was to create a script too, you can bet they'd allocate several months of devising time to do so. Whilst you are unlikely to have this kind of luxury, it's imperative you allocate yourself sufficient time to hone the performance once the text is written. Work on the principle that, when your script is formed, you must rehearse it in the same manner you would a conventional text. Even if your devised piece is not text-based, you should aim to have a script that can be followed, even if it is a map of the play's action or a list of stage directions (look at Beckett's *Act Without Words I* or *Breath* as examples). Give yourself time to sharpen the performances. The best actors are often memorable because their work is detailed; they put sufficient time and thought into creating a role. So, whilst this book provides building blocks, you still need to employ traditional rehearsal methods to hone your devised performances.

A Note on Examples

Throughout the book you will find examples of plays used to demonstrate principles, techniques and exercises. Most are examples from known texts – plays like *The Rivals* and *The Cherry Orchard* – rather than from devised plays. This is in no way a judgement of their respective value, but simply a practical decision. Many devised plays do not have published scripts. Often they are ensemble pieces and physical, practical works. I have chosen, for the most part, to use examples of texts accessible to the reader to demonstrate principles of form, style and story. After all, classics tend to become classics because they work. In many ways, an understanding of these great plays – and how these games might be used to develop and deepen that understanding of them – provides an excellent foundation for the creation of new, devised work.

A Note on Authorship

Aristotle suggested there are six elements that make up drama. There is also a theory that there are seven basic plots; that every story ever written is a derivation of one of these prime narratives, nothing is truly an original construction. The game *Archetypes* (Game 26) explores the idea that every character has its roots in one of six basic personas.

It would, I am sure, be fair to suggest a similar rule for drama games. There are infinite varieties of basic favourites like *Zip, Zap, Zoom!*, otherwise known as *Whoosh!*, *Bing, Bang, Bong!*, ad infinitum. Games are constantly reworked, recycled and reimagined to suit the players, their originators long forgotten. Whilst most of those classic games can be found in my first book *Drama Games for Classrooms and Workshops*, there are still some well-known favourites included here. Others I have gathered over time from other sources, friends, from workshops and from rehearsing with such imaginative practitioners as Max Stafford-Clark, Katie Bonna and Tony Graham, amongst others. Whilst I have invented many of the games, they are undoubtedly inspired by others, and will now be reinvented and adapted further as they are added into the great melting pot of current practice.

ACKNOWLEDGEMENTS

Writing acknowledgements for a book of games is not unlike concocting an elaborate dinner and then trying to work out the precise origin of every individual ingredient, so varied and multifarious are the sources. I have spent most of my life participating in drama classes, whether as a child, as an actor or as a director, and the games in these pages stem from these formative experiences.

I am therefore indebted to all my teachers and to my colleagues, in particular to Mike Leigh and Max Stafford-Clark, who taught me that drama games are as relevant in a professional rehearsal context as they are in a classroom; in fact, that games can be an absolute foundation stone in the development of a new play.

I would particularly like to thank the students I have worked with at Central School of Speech and Drama, RADA and East 15, who tried and tested many of these games. Many thanks are also due to Matt Applewhite and Nick Hern, for their enthusiasm and support in the construction of this book, and the Drama Games series. Most significantly, I would like to thank the actors of Red Handed Theatre Company, as it is through their willingness to trust me in rehearsals that I have been able to foster these methods; in particular, the casts of *The Belle's Stratagem*, *The Rivals* and *Mad Kings and Englishmen*. Working with open-minded actors who have eagerly embraced each new exercise has not only been essential to the genesis of this material, but provides me with constant inspiration and fulfilment. Their generosity of spirit is remarkable.

STAGE ONE

PREPARATION

At this first stage – **Preparation** – these games encourage you to have fun, to let your proverbial hair down and to savour the company of the ensemble. Never underestimate the value of enjoyment in the rehearsal room; it is surprising how much the spirit of rehearsals affects the genesis of the work.

The first few games in this chapter are energetic warm-ups. *Hammertime!* is an energy-fuelled game inspired by MC Hammer's classic '90s tune; *Big Booty* requires the players to get into the groove; *Four Square* is a game of speed; and *Flying Sheep* is, frankly, just daft. The next games, *Synchronicity* and *Robin's Wood*, engender the building of an ensemble, whilst the final five games – *Free Association*, *Doctor Damage*, *Master and Slave*, *Coward's Adverbs* and *Scary Mary* – require players to begin flexing their imaginative muscles in readiness to move onto Stage Two: Generation.

Hammertime!

A nod to MC Hammer's popular '90s hit, 'U Can't Touch This', this is a quick-fire version of a circular warm-up game. It's Hammertime!

How to Play

This game requires players to pass the energy around the circle. This particular game is enjoyable because it encourages everyone to 'bust some moves' and celebrate the best of '90s pop. If you don't know the song, look up the video on YouTube and you will understand the game immediately!

Players stand in a circle. Begin by passing a '*Na!*' around the circle to the left. To do this, simply swing your arm across your body, as if moving to the beat, saying '*Na!*' as you do so. You may choose to listen to the original track for inspiration ('*Na na na na, na na, na na, can't touch this!*'). Pass this movement energetically from player to player all the way around the circle for practice. You must always swing your arm across your body in the direction the '*Na!*' is travelling in.

Now introduce the second rule. To change the direction of the '*Na!*', you say '*Rewind*' (think Ali G), whilst making a pointing gesture back in the direction that the '*Na!*' came from. This sends the '*Na!*' back the other way.

To pass the '*Na!*' across the circle, gesture to someone on the other side of the ring, sticking your arm out towards them making a stopping gesture, hand out, and say '*Can't touch this!*' Make it clear who you are aiming at, so they can then pass the '*Na!*' round.

Once you have mastered these rules, you can add others for more advanced players. Firstly, to skip a player, say '*Pump up the volume!*', pushing your arms up in the air. The '*Na!*' skips your neighbour and passes to the next person in the circle.

Secondly, you can cause the whole circle to break up, move around and reconvene. When it is your turn, say '*Break it down*', crossing your arms over your head. At this point, everyone dances around, swapping places, singing the musical break from 'U Can't Touch This' (the '*Oh, oh ohs*' leading up to

'*Hammertime!*'), whilst everyone changes positions and reforms the circle in a different order. Whoever shouted '*Break it down*' then begins the next '*Na!*' to avoid losing the momentum.

Thirdly, you can throw in the wild card. When the '*Na!*' comes to you, you can say '*Stop!*', making a gesture with palm facing down, as if pushing down. Anyone can snatch the '*Na!*' by making a grabbing gesture and saying '*Hammertime!*', before then passing the '*Na!*' on in the conventional method. This is an amusing way to add a little competitiveness, as whoever is quickest gets to carry on.

The Aim of the Game

This game encourages a high level of focus, requires memory skills and gives everyone an opportunity to have a dance!

Variations and Extensions

This game could easily be reworked with any other song. For younger players something from the current charts is certainly one way to play to their own interests.

Developing a Movement Vocabulary

This version of the game originated when I was devising a new play with students at East 15 Drama School. Their production opened in a 1990's rave. I adapted the game from the original *Zip, Zap, Zoom!* to set the tone for rehearsals and to get us thinking about an appropriate movement vocabulary for the period. You could therefore do the same for any other production. For a Noël Coward play, for instance, you could use Charleston moves and lyrics from songs of the era. Or, for a play set in the sixties, like Amanda Whittington's *Be My Baby*, you could use gestures and words from songs like 'Going to the Chapel', which both develops a textural world for rehearsal and encourages a consideration of the characters' aspirations and interests.

Players	Skills
6+	*Energy, Focus, Confidence, Speed, Awareness*

Big Booty

A chanting game that involves energy, rhythm and some booty-shaking!

How to Play

Players stand in a circle. Number yourselves round the circle, the first player being named Big Booty, the next Big Booty Number One, then Big Booty Number Two, etc., until everyone has a number. The chant then goes as follows, and is spoken in rhythm by everyone:

> *Aaah, Big Booty!*
> *Big Booty, Big Booty, Big Booty.*
> *Big Booty, oh yeah,*
> *Big Booty, Big Booty, Big Booty!*

Then Big Booty calls out '*Big Booty Number Three*' or another number of their choice. Whoever has that number then replies with their own number, followed by a number of their choice ('*Number Three, Number Six*'). Everything continues in rhythm, thus building the chant. If a player wants to pass the chant back to Big Booty rather than one of the numbers, they say '*Big Booty*' instead of a number ('*Number Three, Big Booty*'). The idea is never to break the rhythm.

As soon as someone makes a mistake and breaks the rhythm, either by getting muddled or answering too slowly, they get relegated to the highest number in the sequence. Everyone else moves up accordingly, getting one step closer to becoming Big Booty, the ultimate aim. As soon as the relegated player is in place, the chant begins again. Here is an example of a sequence with nine players:

> ALL: Aaah, Big Booty!
> Big Booty, Big Booty, Big Booty.
> Big Booty, oh yeah,
> Big Booty, Big Booty, Big Booty!

BB: Big Booty, number three!

TWO: Number three, number six!

SIX: Number six, Big Booty!

BB: Big Booty, number two!

TWO: Ummm…

Number Two pauses – *'Too slow!'* – so Number Two becomes Number Nine, Nine becomes Eight, Eight becomes Seven, etc., and we begin again…

ALL: Aah, Big Booty! (*etc.*)

The Aim of the Game

This game encourages concentration, rhythm and speed. Players have to be focused in order to remember their new numbers and pick up their cue when it is called. It is also an effective promotion of ensemble momentum, pacing and control.

Variations and Extensions

To add an extra challenge for advanced players, try playing this game whilst walking around the space. It is much harder than you would imagine! It requires the participants to focus on listening to each other whilst continuing the momentum of their movement. It is an unbeatable exercise for ensemble training or preparation for choral work.

Players	Skills
6+	*Energy, Focus, Timing, Confidence, Awareness, Memory*

Four Square

A fun, fast, physical ball game that keeps you on your toes.

How to Play

Use chalk or tape to mark one large square on the floor, approximately 3m by 3m. Now divide this in half horizontally and vertically in order to create four squares, like so:

1 (King)	2
4	3

The top left square is the King's square, and anyone who stands in it is King. The aim of the game is for a player to become King and to hold this position for as long as possible. One player stands in each square, with any extraneous players queuing at one side, waiting to come in.

The King begins with the ball, and bounces it to another player. The other player must bat it to one of the other players, using their hands. And so on. If anyone misses the ball or if it bounces in their square more than once, they are out. If, however, it doesn't land inside the four squares, the person who batted it is out. When someone gets out they leave the four squares and join the back of the queue. All the players below him or her move one place up the ranks (e.g. if 2 gets out, 3 goes to box 2, 4 goes to box 3, the King does not move; one of the waiting players then comes in to fill box 4).

The King always serves and must always do so on a diagonal, i.e. to the player in box 3.

Players must aim to bat the ball into someone's square. If, however, they want to play mean, they can bat the ball straight at the other player and shout '*Cheeky monkey*' as they do so. If it hits them, that player is out. If the hitter forgets to shout '*Cheeky Monkey*' then they are out.

If you are playing with a big group there is no reason why several matches cannot take place simultaneously. Just ensure the squares are not too close together or flying balls can cause no end of problems!

The Aim of the Game

This is an effective physical warm-up which engenders energy and a high level of focus. It is also an enjoyable way to focus on a specific task and get everyone's bodies into gear without worrying about the performance ahead.

+ Softball, chalk or tape	
Players	**Skills**
6+	*Energy, Focus, Control*

Flying Sheep

One of the silliest warm-up games I know, a game that involves jumping over each other and baying at the moon... not for the faint-hearted!

How to Play

Note: It is vital to have both adequate space and responsible players, as the game is fast paced and involves jumping over each other. Try playing in slow motion at first, to get used to gameplay.

Choose one person to be the wolf and another to be the sheep, let's call them Tom and Vicky respectively. Everyone else must find a space and become a rock, crouching down low, heads tucked in, making themselves as small as possible.

The wolf must catch the sheep. Tom must chase Vicky around the room, baying and roaring as dramatically as possible. Vicky, as the sheep, runs away, baaing as she goes. Now, at any point, she can jump over a rock on this mountainous outcrop. When she does so, whoever she jumps over (in this case, Juliet) transforms into the wolf, rising up with a great roar to scare Tom. Meanwhile, Vicky becomes a rock. Tom automatically then becomes the sheep, and runs away from Juliet baaing in terror, whilst Juliet roars after him, until he jumps over another rock and the process repeats itself.

This game can be hilarious fun but do ensure that the rocks remain small and tucked in, for safety's sake. The more character that you apply in this game, the better – the transformation of the rocks into wolves in particular should always be a moment of high drama.

The Aim of the Game

This game will encourage the group to warm up physically, and to bond. It always leads to fits of giggles.

Variations and Extensions

Whist this simple version of the game is usually sufficient to initiate laughter and hilarity, there are various means of developing gameplay to increase the challenges. Firstly, when the game gets going, you can introduce more active players by touching a rock on the back, and they automatically become an additional sheep. If you have sufficient space, you could also add a second wolf to stir up trouble.

If you are playing with younger players and using the game as a means to explore animal physicality, you can easily adapt the context. Move the game to the African savannah, and change the wolves, sheep and rocks into lions, gazelles and meerkat burrows. Change the setting to Hogwarts and play wizards on broomsticks, being chased by Dementors, swooping over Hogwarts' spires. Or create a South Sea version with clownfish, sharks and coral reefs (clown fish must, of course, laugh as they swim away from their pursuers). Encourage the players to come up with their own contexts and characters.

Players	Skills
8+	*Energy, Speed, Control*

Synchronicity

A very simple warm-up encouraging ensemble work, in which you have to perform simple actions as a group.

How to Play

Find a space in the room. Ask the participants to walk around, maintaining awareness of everyone else in the space. You should work towards maintaining a group speed. Once this sense has been established, try the following simple exercises; each encourages a sense of ensemble playing. Working together as a company – without being led by any one individual – is invariably the most challenging aspect of this exercise.

1.   All speed up to a fast-paced walk.

2.   All slow down to a slow-motion walk, before eventually stopping at the same moment.

3.   All sit down simultaneously, then stand up as one, before setting off again.

Once these basic ensemble activities have been mastered, ask the group to try the following more complex challenges.

1.   Everyone go from a fast-paced walk to a simultaneous stop. When everyone feels it is the right moment, set off again at the same time.

2.   Everyone change the movement simultaneously from a walk to a skip/jumping/dancing/movement/style of your choice. You must not discuss this, it must just happen spontaneously, yet simultaneously.

The Aim of the Game

This exercise encourages the group to begin acting as an ensemble. If and when leaders become obvious, deter those confident individuals from acting on their own. Instead, try and encourage everyone to make group decisions. It can often be useful to split the group in half, one half becoming an audience, so they can witness the effectiveness of moving as one. They can also help by pointing out when they see someone leading, as long as they do so kindly.

Variations and Extensions

Using Sound

For a further challenge, you could add sound. See what happens if, whilst walking around, the group share an emotion – e.g. everyone moves from walking and laughing to walking and crying and then back again. Another interesting alternative is to try and hum the same slowly changing note, at all times staying in tune with the other members of the company.

Using Sticks

If you have access to wooden rehearsal sticks (three- to five-foot poles), give each member of the company a stick and work on simultaneous movement with these props. Initially, the group stands in a circle facing clockwise, with the sticks in their right hands. They need to sense when everyone is going to move, and, simultaneously, let go of their stick and move one pace forward, therefore catching the next person's stick before it falls to the ground. If they do not all move at the same moment, the sticks will fall to the ground. Whilst it takes a while to perfect this, it is worth persevering as eventual success is really rewarding!

Having mastered the circle exercise, work on simple movement sequences using sticks and try and perform them with absolute synchronicity.

+ Rehearsal sticks (optional)	
Players	**Skills**
4+	*Focus, Awareness, Ensemble Work*

Robin's Wood

A dramatic version of the game Sardines, *with far more character.*

How to Play

I played this hilarious game with the cast of *The Rivals* in the actor Robin Soans' beautiful woodland near Northampton. This was a perfect, atmospheric setting for this adaptation of the classic game *Sardines* or *Hide and Seek* and had many of us in stitches as we were shimmying up trees and screaming across the fields in an attempt to escape the wolf pack! Do find an open-air, tree-filled space if you can, it adds so much to gameplay.

Count out the same number of straws as there are players. Cut one straw so it is shorter than the rest. Allow everyone to pick a straw. Whoever gets the short straw is the wolf, but must not let anyone else know. Everyone else is a sheep.

Now everyone must run and hide somewhere in the space, including the wolf. Once everyone is hidden, the game begins. The wolf must howl with all his or her might. Then all the sheep must baa, to give a hint at their location. The wolf listens and seeks out one of the sheep – if a sheep is caught (grabbed) by the wolf they must die in the most bloodcurdling, earsplitting manner, so as to be heard by all the other sheep. This sheep is immediately reincarnated as a wolf. Both wolves then set out to find new victims. Sheep are allowed to move wherenever and whenever they like, so long as they baa loudly whenever they hear a wolf howl.

The game continues as the number of wolves steadily increases until there is only one poor sheep left. It is essential that the sheep baa when the wolves howl – even if there is a wolf right next to a fearful sheep, the sheep must still baa or the game could go on ad infinitum! When all the sheep have been transformed into wolves then you may begin again, picking straws to find a wolf successor.

The Aim of the Game

This is a surprisingly tactical game; if the wolves work together as a pack they are far more likely to find the sheep efficiently. For this reason it is an excellent way to explore the art of working as an ensemble.

The game also requires a degree of honesty from the sheep – it is very tempting to baa very quietly to avoid being discovered, but it is the danger of this discovery which gives the game its thrilling edginess.

+ Outdoor space with hiding places, straws	
Players	**Skills**
8+	*Ensemble Work, Quick Thinking*

7

Free Association

A method of generating new starting points for improvisation and devising by making associations that move you away from obvious choices.

How to Play

In a conventional word-association game, someone will begin with a random word, for instance '*cat*'. The next player must say a word associated with this, for instance '*whiskers*'. The next player must then say a word they associate with whiskers (i.e. not necessarily associated with cats), for instance, '*moustache*'. You rapidly move away from the original word and end up with something entirely detached. This game uses a similar process, but is undertaken with other actors as a group exercise.

Collect together a random assortment of objects, or distribute a Post-it note to each player. Either method is equally as effective. Now split the players into groups of four, and designate each group an area. Place a piece of paper in each of the four corners of each group's area. Each player should choose an object from the pile or write a noun of their choice on a Post-it note. They must then place their object/Post-it on one of the pieces of paper each. Ask the players to move on to the next piece of paper. Using the rules of word association, they must write down the first association they make with the object or word they find there. For instance, if Charity finds a map, she might write the word '*treasure*' at the top of the piece of paper.

Repeat this process, so that each actor moves on again, this time making a word association with the latest word on the sheet (when Dave follows Charity he must create a word association from the word '*treasure*', not '*map*'). When all four corners of the room have been visited, the actors bring the four pieces of paper back into the middle. These four terms are now their new stimuli for improvisation.

Within their group, each actor must choose a partner. They then have one minute to create a scene from two of the words provided. After one minute, they must perform their scene to the other pair. Having watched both scenes, the group now have one further minute to combine them to make one scene with all four actors, based on the four associated words.

If there is material in which everyone is interested, use this as a starting point to do 'second generation' research – finding words, images and texts which relate to these found ideas. Then work on further improvisations from there. If there is nothing for development, go back to the beginning and play the game again. The point is that it is a quick-fire way of generating new ideas and material. It should be used as a fun exercise to stretch the group's imagination, encouraging ideas that arise from random starting points, rather than working from a set, pre-agreed theme.

The Aim of the Game

This can be an exciting exercise to use if you are stuck with stimuli that none of the group are excited by. It can help to develop improvisation skills and to find unusual starting points, thinking 'outside the box' rather than following logical patterns of idea development.

+ Objects, paper, Post-it notes and pens	
Players	**Skills**
4+	*Quick Thinking, Imagination*

Doctor Damage

A comic improvisation game in which a crazed doctor and nurse diagnose fantastical illnesses and prescribe wacky cures for their poor, unsuspecting patients.

How to Play

Choose a doctor and nurse from the group. These two should never have made it into the medical profession; they are entirely deficient of skill in every way! They both misdiagnose the simplest of ailments, and prescribe wildly inappropriate remedies for all manner of wacky diseases.

Ask the other players to line up along the edge of the playing space. They are the patients waiting to be seen. The first in line knocks on the imaginary door. The doctor then shouts *'Come in!'* and asks the patient to sit down.

The doctor and nurse question the patient about their symptoms. At any point, either in relation to the symptoms mentioned, or spotting something far more exciting wrong with them, the doctor and nurse must diagnose the patient and embark on treating him or her.

The improvisation should continue until the patient finds a way to leave – they may suddenly feel better, be terrified of the operation the doctor is embarking on, or find another imaginative reason for leaving before the mischievous medical team have done too much damage. When they have left the space, they join the back of the line of patients, thinking of some new symptoms in order to come in again later, as a new patient. Then the next patient knocks on the imaginary door and the game continues.

This game works best when the players really use their imaginations – no ailment is too unlikely. In the past, the demonic doctors have diagnosed everything from the black death and problematic wind to the growth of a face on the back of a head, a third leg or full body hair! Treatment has included the necessary removal of a leg to treat a common cold, abstinence from breathing to treat wind and the insertion of jelly beans in the belly button as a solution for an unwanted pregnancy. Anything is possible and there is certainly plenty of room for comedy here.

The Aim of the Game

There are several benefits to this game, on top of the fun it never fails to deliver. Firstly, it encourages spontaneity in improvisation. Everyone has to react to the facts brought into play by the other improvisers: the doctor and nurse have to react with immediacy having heard the patient's symptoms, whilst the patient needs to react dramatically to the prognosis.

It also encourages players not to 'block' one another, in terms of accepting ideas. For the improvisation to work well, everyone needs to receive each other's offerings and build on them, in order to create an exciting scene in a short amount of time.

Players	Skills
4+	*Improvisation, Imagination, Spontaneity, Quick Thinking*

Master and Slave

A quick improvisation game in which a slave has to respond spontaneously to his master's complaints.

How to Play

This improvisation game follows a simple structure, encouraging actors to think on their feet, responding to variables in the story.

Choose one player to be master, let's call him Victor. He sits on a chair centre stage, with the others facing him, forming an audience. Victor must point at one of the audience members, saying '*Slave!*' in a commanding voice.

The chosen slave, let's call her Cathy, walks into the playing space submissively, bowing at the master's feet, responding '*Yes, master.*'

The following scene then takes place, the players filling in the gaps as creatively as they can. This means both master and slave have to think on their feet, responding to the other's spontaneous ideas. The basic dialogue is as follows:

> MASTER: What have you been doing, slave?
>
> SLAVE: _____, Sir, as you instructed.
>
> MASTER: Then can you explain why _____!
>
> SLAVE: Well…_____
>
> MASTER: But you should have known _____! Shall I forgive you?
>
> SLAVE: Yes you should, because_____

Cathy and Victor choose to fill in the gaps as follows:

> VICTOR: What have you been doing, slave?
>
> CATHY: Cleaning out your pond, Sir, as you instructed.
>
> VICTOR: Then can you explain why, when I went to bed last night, I found hundreds of squirming frogs between my sheets!
>
> CATHY: Well… I heard from the Wise Woman of the West that frog slime is the perfect perfume for attracting the ladies, and I thought it might help you attract a beautiful bride, Sir.

VICTOR: But you should have known that I am allergic to frog slime, and now I have a rash from head to toe! Shall I forgive you?

CATHY: Yes you should, because I have invited your favourite, Lady Gloria Spottyface, around to keep you company, and she loves pimply masters! Now she is so likely to fall in love with you!

The master then decides whether to forgive the slave or not. If the slave is forgiven, they now become the master and the game continues. Alternatively, you can invite two new players up each time.

The Aim of the Game

This game encourages quick thinking and spontaneity, demanding actors to respond with immediacy to the offerings they are given. Don't forget, however, that it uses slave and master personas as a deliberate characterisation challenge – encourage the actors to play these stock roles as vividly as possible. Remove the chair if you want to encourage further physicality.

Look at the *Commedia Dell'Arte* characters for reference. Zanni is the slave, and his masters include Pantalone and Il Dottore.

Players	Skills
4+	*Improvisation, Imagination, Spontaneity, Storytelling*

Coward's Adverbs

This game is played by the irrepressible Bliss family in Noël Coward's Hayfever. *It involves guessing the manner in which the players are acting… a vocabulary-expanding improvisation game.*

How to Play

One player leaves the room; in the spirit of Noël Coward's play, let's call her Sorel. The others then decide on a specific adverb, which they will all attempt to portray. An adverb is an adjective (describing word) which describes a verb (doing word), for instance '*tenderly*', '*coldly*', '*provocatively*'.

Once the group has decided on an adverb, Sorel returns. She then moves around the players, as they perform actions of their choice towards her in the manner of the word. Try and choose a word which the player is likely to know. In *Hayfever*, the characters decide on the rather challenging adverb '*winsomely*' (sweetly or innocently charming). When Sorel re-enters, Judith is first to perform an action. She hands Richard a flower in a winsome manner. Sorel cannot guess the word yet, so Myra attempts to act winsomely, to no avail. Jackie, when asked to play, protests genuinely in such a sweet and charming manner that Sorel guesses the word, not realising of course that Jackie was not even playing!

Hopefully the actors in your group will be more forthcoming. Easy words for initial rounds or younger players include basic emotion or action words – e.g. '*happily*', '*miserably*', '*boldly*', '*slowly*', '*scarily*', '*gently*', '*dramatically*', '*nervously*', '*energetically*'. For more experienced or older players, challenge them to use more complex vocabulary, or words which demand a more thoughtful response – e.g. '*surreptitiously*', '*drearily*', '*provocatively*', '*willingly*', '*jealously*', '*cockily*'.

The Aim of the Game

The aim of this game is for the players to clarify their motivations in performance, and to be able to play a certain quality in a readable manner. For the player guessing, the game demands analytical skills and improves their attention to detail and ability to relate actions to emotions. It is also a useful vocabulary-expanding exercise.

Variations and Extensions

Try playing this game when rehearsing a known scene from a play. This time, everyone should choose his or her personal adverb, which relates to character, and must play the scene in that specific way. New levels of resonance are often discovered here, by playing a scene in a manner that might not otherwise have been considered. At the end of the scene, or at an appropriate stopping point, everyone should guess each other's adverbs and talk about what was discovered.

Players	Skills
6+	*Characterisation, Improvisation, Vocabulary, Analysis, Imagination*

Scary Mary

A speedy rhyming game in which players have to mime adjectives for the Virgin Mary.

How to Play

Players should sit in a semi-circle. Begin the game by asking one of the players – let's call him Jon – to stand facing the group in the image of the Virgin Mary, with a headscarf adorning his head, and his hands in the prayer position. Jon is now Mary.

Jon must show Mary in a particular stance, choosing any describing word that rhymes with Mary. The audience have to guess what kind of Mary he is. Perhaps Jon will show his chest to reveal Hairy Mary, or takes on a Frankenstein's Monster pose as Scary Mary. When someone guesses correctly, they must jump up and become Mary, choosing a new rhyming adjective. Encourage players to be ambitious, adding syllables to increase difficulty. Scary Mary is easy; Contrary Mary, Prairie Mary or Adversary Mary will take some initiative.

Once you have exhausted the many possibilities of Mary, take another character name and try again. Try Vlad (*bad*, *mad*, *jihad*, *Stalingrad* – unsurprisingly political correctness is often disposed of early on in this game), Mikey (*spikey*, *pikey*, *hikey*, *psyche*), Vicky (*sticky*, *hicky*, *picky*), all of which have many possibilities. If necessary, you can allow '*ing*' on the end of a word to make it easier, i.e. Paul could be *bawling*, *trawling* or *sprawling*.

The Aim of the Game

Whilst this might seem like a juvenile game, once you get past the initial couple of easy rhymes it becomes much more challenging and can demand a great deal of mime skill. Performing a readable mime requires simple, clearly defined and well-chosen movements. The game can also encourage players to think about how to communicate abstract ideas.

+ Tea towel or headscarf, other objects	
Players	**Skills**
3+	*Spontaneity, Characterisation, Quick Thinking*

STAGE TWO

GENERATION

During Stage One: Preparation, the group will, I hope, have got to know each other better and have begun to feel comfortable working as an ensemble, energetically and imaginatively.

In this second phase – **Generation** – you will set off on the creative adventure, jumping off into the unknown. Each of the games here provides a starting point for devising. Some of the games, *Impro Bingo* for example, encourage actors to create characters through improvisation. Others – *Whose Shoes?* or *Use Your Loaf*, for instance – use objects as an initial stimulus. Text is another alternative – use games like *Sound of the Underground* or *Bricolage* to explore words from unusual perspectives. If you would rather write your own script from scratch, *Ladies of Letters* and *Snowball* provide fun methods for doing just that. Or use another artist as an inspiration; instead of Shakespeare, pick a painter like Bruegel or Heironymus Bosch – try *Painting by Numbers* as a devising game which uses art as a stimulus.

These are just a host of ideas. Add your own, adapting these games as you wish. Most importantly, feel free to experiment with any stimuli; we are used to treating texts, particularly classical texts, as sacrosanct. In this instance, don't! Pull it apart, reorder it, turn it on its head, wear it, make a sculpture out of it or throw it away if you do not find it inspiring, and find something else. This stage is all about playing imaginatively with ideas and finding objects, themes and creations that genuinely inspire you. Try not to rush decisions at this stage, as the ideas you eventually choose will form the foundation for the rest of the process.

Impro Bingo

A quick-fire improvisation game that encourages players to create characters spontaneously, with an element of chance thrown in for fun! This game was developed by students at Central School of Speech and Drama.

How to Play

On a piece of paper, draw a chart with five columns and five rows, numbering the columns A to D and the rows 1 to 4.

Write character types down the first column, as shown in the diagram opposite, and activities across the top row. For the simplest method of gameplay, you can stop at this point, without writing any further information into the table.

Now ask two actors to take to the floor, let's call them Harry and Rebecca. Ask a member of the audience to choose a letter between A and D for Harry; for instance C, which is 'Painting'. Ask another audience member to choose a number between 1 and 4; for instance 4, which is 'Convict'. Harry must immediately begin improvising a convict who is painting. Repeat this process for your second actor, so that both actors have a character and an activity. After letting them settle in to their improvisations, choose an appropriate point to say '*Go!*' At this point, the two actors have to meld their scenes together, finding a way to make sense of these two contrasting characters coexisting within a scene. For instance, Harry, the painting convict, might be painting a picture of Rebecca, a magician who is stealing some spells (A1). They must do this without conversing, naturally creating a shared scenario. This is a challenge, but tests their abilities to work imaginatively with the random choices they have been allocated.

For a slightly more complex version of this game, you can add emotions in the boxes in the centre of the table. This gives the actors the added factor of a feeling or motivation within their scene. Harry, who was given C4, must thoughtfully paint Rebecca's magician, who is ambitiously stealing a whole book of spells.

Fill in the table with your own words. Be inventive; you can easily choose activities and characters that relate to a theme you are exploring.

	A *Stealing*	**B** *Gardening*	**C** *Painting*	**D** *Eating*
1 *Magician*	Ambitiously	Nervously	Tenderly	Joyfully
2 *Baker*	Provocatively	Scathingly	Sadly	Skillfully
3 *Runaway*	Gently	Cheekily	Jealously	Hopefully
4 *Convict*	Sensually	Angrily	Thoughtfully	Cunningly

The Aim of the Game

This exercise encourages imagination and spontaneity. By giving the actors randomly selected characters you avoid the temptation to match obvious combinations – if asked to play a convict in a scene, it is unlikely you would have chosen to portray him painting thoughtfully. It is therefore an engaging way to begin exploring three-dimensional characterisations, moving away from conventional stereotypes.

It also encourages actors to work together with immediacy, using their creative skills to create unusual scenes, without the common afflictions of planning and discussions!

+ Paper, pen, list of ideas

Players
4+

Skills
Storytelling, Characterisation, Quick Thinking

Bricolage

A tool for exploring a chosen text, this exercise involves creating an ensemble response from a wealth of individual ideas and elements; a virtual collage of collected images, sounds and words.

How to Play

There are several ways of playing this game, depending on whether you want to explore a specific text that is new to the actors, or whether the actors know the material already.

If this is an initial exploration of a text, then prepare, in advance, Post-it notes to stick around the space. On each note write something to stimulate the actor who finds it. Let us use *Macbeth* as an example, imagining that the text has been given to the group as a stimulus for devising. It could be:

- A line or key word from the text: e.g. *'Is this a dagger I see before me?'* or *'Horror, horror, horror!'*
- The name of a character or a character type: e.g. Macbeth, Witch, Traitor
- A theme: e.g. darkness versus light, nature, the supernatural
- An image from the text: e.g. bloody hands, a hovering dagger
- A style of movement, if appropriate: e.g. enchanted, stealth
- A feeling present in the text: e.g. trepidation, ambition, jealousy

Stick these notes all around the room and invite the actors in. They should each move around the space until they find a note. On reading it, they should remove it, sticking it onto their top, and then continue the journey responding to the note in some way. They might simply begin speaking a line in various ways to other actors as they move around. They might, however, choose a more abstract response, to move as darkness or to try and perform the essence of nature.

This should result in an ensemble creation, in which players are performing their individual elements, but these add together to give a group reaction to the various elements of the original text. The results can often be wonderfully thought-provoking. With large groups it can be effective to split the group into two and do it twice, as many ideas can arise from watching others.

In addition, you can have a stack of Post-it notes to hand out as the exercise continues. It can be fun to write several identical notes which give the bearers a mission within the exercise, to capture the King for example, or to form Burnham Wood. This adds an element of surprise, when you realise some people have common knowledge and others are in the dark. You can adapt the game and the instructions in any way you choose; it is extremely flexible.

The Aim of the Game

This exercise is a simple way of provoking a group response to an idea or text without inhibiting the actors with ideas of a final product. If you give the group twenty minutes to create an ensemble piece exploring *Macbeth*, you may well get a dutifully well-performed and well-structured response, but often these planned pieces lack the immediacy and braveness of something that is truly spontaneous. If nothing else, it is an excellent way to tackle a challenging stimulus without getting bogged down in detail.

Variations and Extensions

If the actors are already familiar with the text, you can ask them each to write their own Post-it notes, which they then stick around the room for someone else to find. It can also be fun to suggest that they can steal or swap notes with someone else, in order to keep the picture changing.

+ Pens, Post-it notes	
Players	**Skills**
8+	*Imagination, Analysis, Ensemble Work*

Whose Shoes?

A game exploring the links between costume, physicality and characterisation.

How to Play

This game is incredibly simple and rewarding. Place a box in the middle of the room, and fill it with assorted shoes; the more varied, the better. You can ask actors to bring in a couple of pairs each if you wish.

Ask the players to sit facing the playing space. One by one, players should go up, moving in a neutral fashion, and peer inside the box. They must then take out a shoe. When they put this shoe on, that side of their body becomes inhabited by the shoe's character. For instance, a high heel might give you a feminine, alluring model; a thick-soled black shoe might suggest a policeman. The audience should watch carefully as the actor transforms into the new character.

There are two levels of gameplay:

The Easy Version
> Ask the actors to find two matching shoes and fully inhabit that particular character.

The Challenging Version
> For a greater challenge (and often hilarious results), encourage people to select two contrasting shoes, and enjoy the results as they try to play two characters simultaneously, one on their left side and the other on their right.

Once one actor has had the opportunity to explore the space as their new character, the next actor should go up and choose a shoe. When there are two characters in the space, encourage them to begin interacting non-verbally in character. Continue this until all players have a character.

The Aim of the Game

This game allows players to explore how our manner of walking not only affects posture and physicality, but also helps to define personality. It is a fun way of creating spontaneous and often bizarre characterisations, working from an external stimulus.

Variations and Extensions

Shoe Envy

As an easy and dramatic extension of this game, once all the actors are moving about in character, choose a moment to shout *'Change!'* At this moment, all actors must see a shoe on someone else's foot that they are attracted by. They must then try and swap or steal the shoe, coercing its owner to give it up, perhaps by showing off their own shoe. If they manage to gain someone else's shoes, they must take on the corresponding character. Everyone, at all times, should have a shoe on. Survival of the fittest!

+ Assorted shoes	
Players	**Skills**
6+	*Characterisation, Improvisation, Imagination*

Marbles

A game that breaks down the process of devising from an object, giving you a range of ways to kick-start the creative process.

How to Play

Ask the players to get into teams of two or three. Hand out an object to each group. Simple objects like marbles, toys or household items work well.

Let us imagine that there are five teams of three and we are going to use the same object (a marble) for each group. Give them one minute to silently look at their object, play with it, feel its weight, texture, consider its purpose, its 'backstory'.

Now give each of the five groups one of the following categories – literal, physical, textural, emotional and visual. They have four minutes to create a short scenario (it does not have to be a complete story, more a scene with a sense of purpose or activity). The category gives them the method through which they must create their scene:

Literal Analysis

> The object must be used for its true purpose – create a scene in which the object features as itself and therefore suggests a location, time and concept. E.g. A wartime evacuee gets to know the farm children she has been rehoused with over a game of marbles.

Physical Analysis

> Explore how the object moves, what it does, what are its active qualities? A marble rolls, sometimes in a straight line, sometimes on a curve – try this and see where it leads you. E.g. A scene of monkeys in a zoo, playfully rolling around.

Textural Analysis

> Explore how it feels, what is the quality of the material? Marbles are hard and dense, thick glass with a smooth exterior. How could you create characters or a scenario exploring these qualities? E.g. Three criminals meet under a bridge to plan their crime; one is hard and tough, one is lithe and smooth and the other one is rather dense.

Emotional Analysis

> Explore the emotional response to the object and create a scene from the essence of this emotion (not the object itself). E.g. A marble evokes feelings of play, fun, lack of responsibility, youthfulness, so the scene may feature the journey home of three children on the last day of school before the long summer holidays.

Visual Analysis

> Explore the marble's appearance and its visual qualities. It is shiny, glassy, transparent, has a wave of colour running through it, distorting the view if you look through it. Use these qualities to create characters or a scenario. E.g. An old woman peers deep into a glass mirror at her pale reflection. Her skin is almost translucent, but as she looks she dreams of her younger, bright and jovial self. We watch the scene of her memory replay.

The staggering variety of responses that can be derived from a single object can be fascinating. You can easily play this game with varied objects, but for small groups it is interesting to compare variations on the theme by using identical objects.

The Aim of the Game

The aim is to arm players with a variety of practical tools for devising from an object. It encourages actors to think imaginatively and to appreciate that there are a wealth of paths into the creation of a scene, other than a literal use of an object to create a narrative.

Variations and Extensions

You may choose to add your own categories: the sound of the object, the size, or, to add a little spice, the smell or taste of the object (if appropriate… and edible).

+ Objects	
Players	**Skills**
6+	*Imagination, Analysis, Improvisation, Storytelling, Ensemble Work*

The Detective Game

A devising game in which actors create stories behind the objects.

How to Play

Divide the players into groups of about four. They are the detectives, and it is their task to solve the mystery behind the 'discovery'. Now hand out the discoveries, one per group. This could be any object, but preferably one with personality (a furry stole, a wallet, or a decorative jewellery box are more interesting choices than a pencil or a blank piece of paper, for example).

They must first pass the object around their group, inspecting it closely for clues. Then they must give their analysis of what the object is and the story behind it. They should remember, as detectives, that they need to give a convincing analysis. This does not mean, however, that it cannot be bizarre or fantastic. Once they have discussed their own stories, they should present them to the other groups. Line four chairs up as a panel, and the detectives then deliver their theories.

For example, the presentation by the group analysing the fur stole might go something like this:

TIM: Well, fellow detectives, this article belonged to Lady Offwell, who was found murdered on her tennis courts last night. You can see by the way the fur falls that this was undoubtedly the murder weapon.

BEN: What rot! This is clearly the shed skin of the rare but deadly Quat, a terrifying beast which threatens our peaceful neighbourhood.

ROSS: You are both wrong, detectives. This is, without a doubt, one of the missing relics from the Great Museum Robbery of 1889.

GEORGE: I will tell you what it is. This fur is the cursed headdress of the voodoo woman Lashalot, this town's most wanted criminal!

The audience must vote, by a show of hands, on which story they think is most interesting and has the most potential. If a couple of stories are equally popular, you can give them the challenge of combining the two. Then give all the groups time to devise their piece. You can either set them off to work at their own pace, or break down the process by asking them to create a tableau of the scene described, then create 'before' and 'after' tableaux, in order to establish the structure of their story. Finally, the playlets should be presented to the whole group.

The Aim of the Game

This simple devising exercise allows players to devise a narrative directly from a prop without 'overthinking' it. Giving the decision-making power to the audience reduces discussion time and encourages the players to think about what makes an intriguing scenario.

+ Objects	
Players	**Skills**
4+	*Imagination, Storytelling*

Use Your Loaf

An hilarious game that encourages players to use objects inventively.

How to Play

Object manipulation – the use of props or found objects as something other than their obvious purpose – is a highly creative way of devising short scenarios and playing with theatrical concepts.

In this exercise we use loaves of bread because they are malleable and destructable, but also because we associate loaves with the everyday. We see them in our houses each morning, on our breakfast tables, and, as a result, there is something particularly pleasurable about subverting this symbol of routine, doing something different with it, and going against the grain (no pun intended).

Everyone stands in a circle. Pass the loaf to the first player, let's call her Harriet. She must begin a solo improvisation in which the loaf becomes a new object.

A loaf's natural malleability can be taken advantage of here – Harriet should feel free to rip it, pull a bit off, break it in two, whatever she wants, as long as it serves her improvisation.

For example, Harriet says '*Oh no, where are my keys?*' and promptly rips open the top of the loaf. She has chosen to use it as a handbag. She continues to pull bits of the loaf out as she frantically searches her 'bag' for her keys, spraying pieces of bread onto the floor (this is fine). She pulls out one particularly chunky morsel of bread: '*Aha! Found them,*' she says, before passing the loaf (now rather hollow), onto the next player, Katie.

Katie must use the remaining loaf as a totally new object. As the bread gets passed from player to player, it decreases in size, therefore making the game more challenging.

The Aim of the Game

This game always feels like a release. It allows players to be rather reckless with an object, destroying it in the process, which engenders a certain freedom.

It is a quick way of exploring object manipulation, and is an unusual yet effective way of encouraging actors to think imaginatively. The focus is not on creating scenes so much as engendering in the participants the confidence to use objects in inventive ways. Why does a loaf of bread have to be a mere loaf of bread? The rule is there are no rules.

+ Several whole loaves of bread	
Players	**Skills**
4+	*Imagination,* *Object Manipulation*

Ladies of Letters

A narrative-development exercise in which players create characters quickly using the written word. It is inspired by the BBC Radio 4 drama of the same name.

How to Play

Before you begin, set the same number of piles of paper around the room as there are players. There should be four sheets in each pile. Each player needs a pen.

Ask all the players to walk around the space, walking with purpose and energy. When you say '*Stop!*', they must walk to a pile of paper and sit next to it. Now ask them to '*Begin writing!*' They have three minutes to conceive of a scenario and write a persuasive letter from one character to another. The letter writer might ask for something specific, for a favour or for something more abstract, for advice or to be part of a scheme of some kind. They must write in vocabulary and using phrasing suited to their choice of character, considering age, education, formality, persuasive tactics, etc. For example, Natalie writes a letter from Amelia, the maid, to Cuthbert Fennington-Smythe, the rich owner of the house, asking for time off to visit her sick mother. She writes colloquially, using simple vocabulary and local diction.

After three minutes say '*Stop!*' (give the group a thirty-second warning). Everyone should fold up their letters, as if ready to post, write the addressee's name on the outside and then leave it on top of the pile. They must then jump up and walk around the space again until you shout '*Stop!*' At this point they must go to the pile nearest them and read the letter they find there.

After adequate reading time, ask them to '*Begin writing!*' They have three minutes to write a response, in character, to the letter they have found. Jenny, who picks up Natalie's letter, writes back to Amelia as Cuthbert. However, the writer must 'raise the stakes' each time, finding greater drama in the situation. Rather than just replying yes or no, what can Jenny do to make the situation more dramatic? For example, Cuthbert might agree, but only if Amelia agrees to marry him, as he has been in love with her since she first arrived and is desperate to be with her, despite their class differences.

After three minutes repeat the process, until four letters have been written. In the third round, the player writes back as the first character (Amelia), raising the stakes again. Amelia might, for example, say yes, as she admits she is in love with him too, but she has a fiancée, Edward, whom she cannot escape from. In the final round, the last letter must conclude the scenario. For example, Cuthbert tells Amelia that he will challenge Edward to a duel, or perhaps forms a plot to poison him stealthily, in order to be with her.

Once all four letters have been written you can either share them with the group, reading them out as if a conversation, or converting them into a script. Alternatively, you can split into groups to dramatise the stories.

The Aim of the Game

The aim is two-fold. Firstly, the exercise encourages players to explore the way in which words inform characterisation. Secondly, it is an ideal opportunity to explore the importance of raising the stakes in storytelling.

Look at the construction of any well-loved story and identify the points at which the pressure is added to by increasing the level of risk. A group of boys play in the wood, but then they get lost, then it gets dark, then they get separated, then the solo boy remembers the dark and dangerous beast who lurks in this forest…

+ Paper, pens	
Players	**Skills**
4+	Characterisation, Storytelling, Writing, Vocabulary

Sequences

A structured way of creating movement sequences, this is a physical devising method, which encourages action before narrative.

How to Play

Note: Try and complete this exercise in silence. It is infinitely more focused without unnecessary chat and tends to lead to more creative results.

Ideally, all the participants will need a rehearsal stick, a long, blunt-ended wooden pole about three to five foot long. If preferable they could substitute a chair or a piece of material, or they can complete the exercise without an object.

Ask each player to find a space. Give everyone one minute to explore the properties of their stick. In this time they should move with it, test out positions, explore their relationship with the object, etc.

After one minute of exploration time, allow the players a further minute to arrive at four frozen poses, using their poles. Consider use of all the planes of space – use the floor, horizontal lines, vertical lines, the proximity between pole and body, explore the contrast between poses, etc.

Then allow one final minute for the participants to solidify their four poses. They must know them well enough to teach them to others, maintaining an awareness of where each limb should be, how tense the pose is, each of the angles, etc.

Ask everyone to find a partner, let's call ours Tim and Sam. Tim must now teach Sam his four moves without talking – this is sequence A. Next, Sam must teach Tim his four moves, still in silence – this is sequence B.

Once both partners know all eight moves, they must decide how to perform them. They might both perform the sequences one after the other, A followed by B. Will they face each other, will they face the same direction? Will one of them put the sequence on a different axis (e.g. Tim might perform his horizontally and Sam vertically). In terms of sequence, perhaps Tim will perform AB and Sam, BA. Perhaps a narrative sense will emerge, an emotion – is this a battle? A dance of seduction?

Give the pair enough time to practise their sequence and then watch some of them. Look at the contrasts in the results. It is always interesting to see that some pieces have become heavily narrative, others like a dance with a sense of flow between each move, others rather robotic.

Ask each pair to find two other pairs, to form groups of six. Ask them to find a configuration in which they can perform their three pieces as one. Give them several minutes to work on staging, to consider whether all three pieces run with the same tempo or dynamics, and to investigate interaction. Do partners stay next to each other or start at opposite ends of the space? Does what one pair does affect another? Is there an overriding theme or narrative? What kind of picture is being created?

Having watched the results, you may wish to split the whole group in half and to form two new performances. It can be interesting, at this stage, to allow one group to speak to each other, whilst banning talking for the other group.

It may seem strange to ban talking but if the focus is on action and concentration then working without words often produces better, even more inventive results. It removes debate and encourages teamwork.

The Aim of the Game

The aim is to use action as a route for generating material. So often we focus on using our heads to make work – think of a scenario, think of a story… In this exercise the narrative pressure is off – it is about creating unrelated and often random poses, then lacing them together. If a narrative naturally evolves from the interaction between people, actions and objects, then great; but if not, enjoy the beauty of abstraction and the interest created by allowing the audience to form their own opinions on what they are witnessing.

+ Rehearsal sticks, chairs or lengths of fabric	
Players	**Skills**
6+	Physicality, Storytelling, Memory, Ensemble Work

Sound of the Underground

A means of generating characters and material from text.

How to Play

Split the actors into groups of four, and distribute a random text to each group. Ideal texts are not those from which you would expect to draw a narrative. Choose something unusual and interesting to look at on the page. The London Underground map is ideal because it has a plethora of unusual words and names, whilst also having an interesting layout.

Give the groups one minute for the first task, in which each player must choose a word from the text. If using the London Tube map, for example, Cian, Sam, Celia and Ella might choose '*Monument*', '*Oval*', '*Kennington*' and '*Crescent*' (as in Mornington Crescent). Each must then write their word at the top of their piece of paper, then hand it on to another member of the group.

Give everyone one minute to write a sentence for the word they have been given.

> Cian writes: 'Nights pass, mornings pass, dew settles and the green lichen now covers its stone curves, but the monument still stands.'

> Sam writes: 'The oval glinted brightly.'

> Celia writes: 'Kennington was a sprightly young officer. If it wasn't for his unfortunate plague of acne, he would have been all the girls' favourite the day the troops returned.'

> Ella writes: 'The crescent moon rose high into the early April sky, shedding a luminous light.'

These sentences then form the starting point for a scene. Give the group three minutes to read their phrases and to look for links. Consider the images in the text, any suggestion of characters, period, themes. Whilst sometimes the sentences fit together coherently, other groups will find some hilarious contrasts in their sentences and might initially feel stumped. It is often the groups with the most challenging collection of sentences who come up with the most engaging work.

Ask the group to create four tableaux from the sentences. They might choose to create a tableau of each sentence, or, having discovered more of an overview, they might present four images from an emerging narrative. The purpose of asking for still images is to keep the focus on the images and emotions that the text evokes rather than pushing hurriedly towards a narrative for the sake of creating a story.

Once the group has arrived at four tableaux, share these with the other groups and ask the audience what they can read from these pictures. This can often kick-start further ideas for scenes which the group had not anticipated.

Having received their feedback on their tableaux, give the groups between five and ten minutes to generate a short scene.

The Aim of the Game

This method of devising encourages players to steer away from obvious scenarios when creating scenes. By working from a random text they will arrive at a disparate collection of words, then phrases, and will have to think more creatively to find links between them. Often the resulting work is original and engaging. It is also a way of exploring non-script-based texts as a starting point.

+ Paper, pens, source texts	
Players	**Skills**
6+	Analysis, Ensemble Work, Storytelling, Writing

Snowball

An exercise in which you quickly generate scenarios by adding new elements to a 'snowball' thrown around the space.

How to Play

Give each player a piece of paper and a pen and ask them to find a space to sit in the room. They have thirty seconds to write a short description of a character at the top of the piece of paper. The more descriptive the statement, the easier the character will be to play later on. For instance, Tony creates 'Puddingbeard, a peg-legged pirate who tries to be tough but who is terrified of women'.

After thirty seconds, ask them to fold their statement over so it cannot be seen, then screw up the piece of paper (like a snowball) and throw it to someone else in the room. When everyone has caught a snowball, ask the players to unravel their ball, leaving the top section folded (they must *not* read the first character description). They then write a description of a second character. Let's imagine that Becky caught Tony's snowball. She writes 'Esme, a bolshy tomboy from Lewisham who wants to be a rap artist'.

When this is completed, continue the exercise for two more rounds, keeping the previous information folded out of sight throughout. Each round, the snowball should be thrown to a new player. In round three, players must write a description of a location – e.g. 'a desert island' – and in round four, a simple dilemma – e.g. 'How are you going to deliver the baby?'

After these four rounds, when all four elements have been written, everyone must toss their snowballs in the air simultaneously, and try to catch one. Then ask the players to get into pairs. Now they can unravel both sheets and read the four elements on each. There are several alternative approaches to using these starting points. Either give the pairs five minutes on each scenario, asking them to build a scene from one, then repeat the exercise to develop the second scenario. Alternatively, you may ask them to choose their favourite of the two to work on, or ask them to make a hybrid of the two. Whichever you choose, the results are often both unusual and highly imaginative!

Using our example, the players create a scene in which the nervous Puddingbeard is left to supervise Esme, who has been taken captive (and is particularly narked by the situation) whilst the other pirates explore the desert island. She then goes into labour, and Puddingbeard has to face his phobia of females to help her deliver the new baby, who is then crowned King of the island, and Esme raps at the coronation.

The Aim of the Game

This exercise encourages players to work with other people's ideas, accepting the factors they are given and creating short scenarios spontaneously. It also requires players to explore the benefits (and sometimes drawbacks) of detailed description, and to observe the importance of a dilemma in making an engaging scene.

+ Paper, pens	
Players	**Skills**
6+	*Imagination, Writing, Storytelling*

Site Specifics

An exercise in which you use the nature of the space you are working in as a starting point for generating material.

How to Play

There are many ways in which you can use a specific site as a starting point for the development of new work. Here are a few simple exercises to generate thoughts.

Begin in the rehearsal room, using the following exercises to explore this familiar space. Firstly, ask the group to explore the *length* of the space. They can take this instruction to mean whatever they want, but are free to move around. They should do this silently. After a minute or so, ask them, as a group and without talking, to take a position that reflects the length of the space. By asking them not to communicate vocally they are likely to give a more instinctive response.

Once they have done so, ask them to explore the *height* of the space. This is considerably more tricky, but might engender some engaging modes of movement as they explore the dynamic of height. Once again, ask the group to come up with a position that reflects the height of the space, without talking.

The next categories are somewhat more abstract, and will often lead to more complex and engaging results. Ask the group to explore the *shape* or *size* of the space, the *energy* of the space, the *atmosphere* or *character* of the space, and the *history* of the space. Depending on where you are working you may get some relatively literal results (a church hall may give you ghosts and religious ceremonies); others are far more metaphysical. It is the contrast in individual responses that often leads to interesting results. Each time ensure you allow the actors time to explore the space on their own, then ask them to create a group response.

There are several ways in which you can use this generated material. Ideally, split everyone into groups and send them off to find an interesting space in the vicinity. They should then follow the exercises above, as demonstrated in the rehearsal room, to explore their chosen space. Allow them time to manipulate their responses into a short two-minute piece, which they can share with the other groups. You can explore the idea of location by showing the pieces both back in the rehearsal room and in the spaces where they were devised. The differences between the two are often fascinating. If it is not suitable to send groups off to other areas, you can always ask them to create a two-minute sequence using anything they found interesting from their collective responses in the rehearsal room, then share these with the other groups.

The Aim of the Game

The aim is to encourage the actors to respond organically to the location they are working in. If they find this interesting, they may well want to further explore the idea of site-specific or site-sensitive work, or look at locations as a starting point for narrative.

Players	Skills
6+	*Imagination, Physicality, Ensemble Work, Analysis*

Red Riding Hood and the Loaded Gun

An exercise that forces players to cope with unexpected added factors within stories they know well.

How to Play

Split the group into teams with a minimum of three players. Ask each group to choose a story that they are familiar with. It could be a myth (like St George and the Dragon), a fairy tale or a popular modern story. Ask each group to sit in a circle and retell the story to each other to ensure they all know it well and are thinking about the same version.

The groups need to establish the beginning, middle and end of their stories – they should be able to summarise each phase in one sentence. This becomes the title of each section of the story.

Ask them to write each title on a separate piece of paper. Write the title clearly at the top of each sheet and illustrate it below (like a storyboard). For example, a group who chose *Little Red Riding Hood* might title their first picture 'Red Riding Hood travels through the wood to Grandmother's house'. The pictures should illustrate the events in as much detail as possible in a couple of minutes. When completed, stick the three sheets to the wall.

Now the fun begins! Ask the groups to move around to the next group's pictures. Give them several minutes to think of a way to throw a proverbial spanner into the works of this familiar story. They are allowed to make edits to two out of the three pictures. They can either change the titles or draw something in the picture. Ask them to think inventively. Perhaps, in the first picture of Red Riding Hood they could add something to her basket… Cyanide? A pistol? A love note to the wolf? A ransom note for Grandmother? It should be something that adds drama. Alternatively, they can make a textual edit, for example, editing 'Red Riding Hood travels through the wood to Grandmother's house' might be edited to become 'Red Riding Hood time-travels to Grandmother's house'.

Once each group has made two edits, ask them to go back to their original storyboards. They must edit their own third picture in order to make a complete story. Give them ten minutes to create a dramatic rendition of their storyboard. This can often have hilarious results.

The reason for only allowing two edits is that it puts the onus on the original group to pull the story together cohesively. They need to work with the extra factors to create a clear and fluid narrative. It is usually easiest if the final picture has been left unedited. However, often the most interesting stories are those where the original group has to form a new beginning to make sense of the unusual events, or work out an engaging link between an unconventional beginning and ending.

The Aim of the Game

This exercise encourages experimentation with established stories, using them as springboards for creativity. The exercise is intended to dispel the myth that any idea is too ridiculous. Undoubtedly the groups will challenge each other by adding bizarre factors into each other's stories. The players have to work with whatever they are given, and by doing so will gain confidence in their ability to stage any story, no matter how outrageous.

+ Paper, pens	
Players	**Skills**
6+	Imagination, Storytelling, Ensemble Work

Painting by Numbers

An exercise in which you work from a painting to create scenarios.

How to Play

Firstly, choose a painting that is full of life – a Bruegel painting is ideal, as his work is peopled with figures. Hieronymus Bosch is ideal if you want to stretch the players imaginatively, as his dark and bizarre images are full of mysterious creatures and dramatic scenes. If your devised piece is to be set in a particular era, then consider looking at paintings from the period, as it encourages you to explore the world of the play. I used Hogarth prints, for example, in rehearsal for Nell Leyshon's play *Bedlam*, as the pictures depict the gruesome realities of life in mental institutions in the mid-1700s, the setting of the play.

Before you begin work with the actors, you will need to decide how to divide up the painting. I have often divided paintings neatly into numbered quarters or eighths (depending on how many groups you have) and then ask each group to pick a number. You can, if you would rather, give them free reign and ask them to pick their own part of the picture to investigate, or ask them to bring in pictures which they are interested in themselves.

Ask each group to spend some time looking at their portion of the picture. The first exercise is to ask them to improvise the part of the scene they see. Give them some time to consider who these people are, what their intentions are and what has just happened. Their scenario should be no more than a minute long.

Now divide the groups into two – the players and the audience. Pick one group from the players to perform their scene. After thirty seconds, ask another group of players to go up and perform theirs simultaneously. You might get interaction between the scenes, you might not. Continue to add scenes until all groups are part of the action. You will, in effect, have created a living version of this painting. Watch carefully to see how dynamics develop and how stories evolve as groups interact.

Afterwards, ask the audience to report back on what they saw. What was most interesting dramatically? Depending on the findings, the players could then build on their individual scenes or combine with other groups to create an ensemble piece.

The Aim of the Game

This game can be used both to generate new material and to give access to a particular period or theme, which leads to further work. We often respond to images in a more immediate and playful way than text, which can sometimes engender a rather academic approach.

Variations and Extensions

Consider picking two related or contrasting paintings for the two halves of the group in order to then create a dramatic clash when mixing the groups up. Medieval frescoes that depict Heaven and Hell can be particularly interesting as they are both emotive and detailed.

Alternatively, work on a similar theme but in contrasting styles. You might, for example, explore lust or greed by choosing one of Banksy's graffitied images depicting images of modern consumerism.

+ Copies of paintings, paper, pens

Players	Skills
8+	*Imagination, Analysis, Ensemble Work, Improvisation, Characterisation*

Merry-Go-Round

A quick game in which players must improvise in pairs around a set theme.

How to Play

Think of an idea you would like to explore and choose five or so related scenarios for pairs.

Ask each player to find a partner and name themselves A and B. Ask As to stand in a circle. Bs then make an inner circle, standing facing their partners.

Announce the first improvisation title, allocating a specific role for A and B. Each improvisation should run for one minute only. The actors must think on their feet. There is no discussion. Choose scenarios that relate to the piece you are devising. For example, in preparation for the devised play *Mad Kings and English Men*, a comical history of England, we began with the following: '*A is a teenage William Shakespeare looking for inspiration and B is Christopher Marlowe, the school bully... Go!*'

The actors have sixty seconds to play out this scene before you shout '*Change!*' The A players then move clockwise around the circle to stand opposite a new partner. Now shout out the second improvisation scenario, for example: '*A is a frustrated Queen Matilda, who has been locked in a tower, and B is her maid, trying to keep her entertained... Go!*'

If you choose, you can always pause the merry-go-round between scenarios in order to watch some of the scenes.

The Aim of the Game

The aim of this game is to create quick-fire spontaneous scenes, some of which might be starting points for further work. It is a great way of exploring a concept or theme, and it's always fascinating to see how original scenes are when they are not overly prepared – in improvisation it is better not to plan, just do it!

Players	Skills
6+	*Imagination, Spontaneity, Focus*

STAGE THREE

EXPLORATION

In Stage Two: Generation, you will hopefully have found a host of ideas that interest you. Perhaps you have characters in mind. You might have found a theme, a question, a period that inspires you, or developed some mini-scenes or pieces of writing you want to develop. This next stage – **Exploration** – encourages you to do just that. The aim here is to investigate that world and to begin constructing firmer ideas, sketching characters and story and considering the qualities and form of your piece.

The games in this section are designed to delve deeper into your initial ideas. Some games investigate the qualities of character – *Archetypes* and *Humour Quad*, for example, give actors the tools to investigate the elements which make up a personality. Other games explore genres of performance and structural options, encouraging actors to test out a range of possible performance styles rather than opting for an obvious naturalistic, linear piece. Playing *Style Wars*, actors can perform the story in a whole range of alternative performance modes, whilst in *Rewind* and *Role Reversal* they will play with the structure and given aspects of the piece. Other games investigate dramatic conventions – *Match Point*, *Convention Conundrum* – whilst some promote a more detailed approach to characterisation and status levels – *Animal Instincts*, *Stan's Game*, *Hydra*, *Sir Anthony!*

Throughout this phase a clearer overview of the piece should emerge. It is still a generative stage, but as you play, keep a constant eye on interesting discoveries. Make a note of engaging material, focus on the narrative, develop the characters and consider the style of performance. There is still plenty of time to hone detail, but be brave in making choices now to allow you time to breathe life into those aspects which you are truly excited about.

Archetypes

A game in which we use classical character archetypes to experiment with our given characters.

How to Play

According to classical theories of drama, there are six 'archetypes' or basic characters. Every character in literature could, it was supposed, be identified as some combination of the following six personas:

> KING – *dominant*
>
> MOTHER – *nurturing*
>
> HERO – *headstrong*
>
> TRICKSTER – *cunning*
>
> INNOCENT – *inquisitive*
>
> FOOL – *loyal/unwise*

Each archetype is genderless and ageless, and there is no judgement attached. The Trickster, for example, is not necessarily a bad character, nor the King good; do not make the mistake of taking them too literally. The archetypes simply reveal the energy and motivation of each character.

Use these as a means to investigate your characters as follows. Ask the actors to find a space. Work through each of the six archetypes and ask everyone to take a pose and find a sound which represents the energy and quality of each archetype. Look at the varying placement of the energy of the sound and the gesture – we use a chest voice and forward energy for the Hero, and a loftier head voice and rather more hesitant energy for the Innocent, for example.

Ask the group to work in pairs, choosing someone they have a scene with. If there aren't scenes yet then improvise an encounter between two characters. They should choose the two archetypes that they feel their character is most obviously a combination of. Hamlet, for example, is perhaps an Innocent Hero or a Trickster Hero; Claudius might be a Trickster Fool; perhaps Old Hamlet (the Ghost) is a Mother King (remember age and status are irrelevant, this is to do with personality and the Ghost has both parental traits and regal qualities). The pair work on their scene, attempting to communicate the two archetypes in their performance, using their energy, physicality and a clear sense of what drives them. Then perform these scenes to the rest of the company, who must guess which two archetypes were chosen.

Now, and often more interestingly, the pairs repeat the scene but choose two other archetypes. Then work through it a third time with the remaining two. More often than not one of the less obvious options will seem surprisingly apt, and the actors might discover new aspects of their characters. Each member of the company finally decides, having tried all three combinations of archetypes (and therefore all six) which two are, in actual fact, their most dominant. It will often be different from the two they first supposed.

The Aim of the Game

This is a rather liberating way to explore new angles of established characters. By using archetypes we stop worrying about interpretative decisions we have made, and so can experiment freely within these new parameters. It also encourages actors to think about what motivates their character, and what are their overall objectives.

Players	Skills
Any number	Analysis, Improvisation, Characterisation, Physicality

Hydra

A game that uses verbatim theatre-making techniques by interviewing many people – many talking heads – to generate characters.

How to Play

This is an exercise used regularly by director Max Stafford-Clark in the development of verbatim plays, including David Hare's *The Permanent Way* and Robin Soans' *Talking to Terrorists*, for his theatre company Out of Joint.

Verbatim theatre uses real testimony, often word for word, as a script. The writer, and often members of the creative team, conduct interviews with participants, transcribing their words and then carefully editing these testimonies to create a final script.

In this exercise, the group creates an ensemble response to an interview, in order to reflect each of their different responses to what was heard, and to paint as full a picture as possible of the interviewee.

Working in groups of four or five, the first task is to find someone to interview. Find someone who is not known well to the actors; perhaps a theatre technician, or, in a school, a teacher or other member of staff. Set a chair facing the interviewers. The group have ten minutes to ask this person any questions they would like to. They must listen carefully, trying to remember as much detail as possible and avoid writing anything down. In a 'real' verbatim situation, they would document the interview, either writing it down or (better) recording it, but for this exercise focus on listening and observing. They must watch the interviewee's mannerisms hawkishly, listen to their tones and their manner of speaking. Once they have adequate material, they should thank the interviewee and let them go.

Now the group must recreate the interview. One player should 'play the group' asking the questions, and all the others must communally play the interviewee. They must sit next to each other and individually physicalise the interviewee as specifically as possible. They can reply together where necessary, and add detail to each other's answers as they remember them. Note how some elements will have been particularly memorable, and everyone will take part in recreating those moments.

Once this exercise is completed, everyone should consider the kind of details they found most interesting and why. More often than not it will be small details that sprang out; we tend to be more drawn in by the minutiae in stories as we can relate to them. Whilst Alecky Blythe and Adam Cork's innovative verbatim musical *London Road* explores the repercussions of five murders in Ipswich, it is the detailed observations of real life that allow us to relate to the characters; for instance, the importance of selecting the right flowers to enter a neighbourhood hanging-basket competition. Remember this if you decide to devise a verbatim piece.

The Aim of the Game

This exercise is intended to help actors explore the multiple facets of character. It also provides a tool for generating new material and is an ideal starting point for any group making verbatim theatre. In this case, you can make your interviews issue-specific, and choose your interviewees accordingly.

It also offers a means of observing truthful emotional delivery. Anyone who performs a monologue in a play or for an audition will, most likely, have to recount dramatic events as part of the text. Note how the emotion in telling a story often contrasts to the emotion felt at the time; people often recount troubling or emotional stories with a measure of humour to make them easier to retell.

Players	**Skills**
4+	Analysis, Awareness, Memory, Characterisation, Ensemble Work

Style Wars

A game that allows you to experiment with the genre and style of the performance within your already-established story.

How to Play

Use this game to explore a potential storyline. If you do not have a story yet you could pick a well-known folk tale or story from a newspaper instead.

Firstly, the group must break their story down into six points and write each point on a prompt card, before handing them back to you.

Hand out blank prompt cards and ask the group to brainstorm styles or genres of performance. They must then write each style on a prompt card. If you are playing this game with drama students, they might like to use particular practitioners like Brecht or Stanislavsky – a handy bit of revision. Some suggestions of styles are:

> *Hammer Horror*
> *Melodrama*
> *Silent Movie*
> *Naturalism*
> *Detective Story*
> *Romance*
> *Opera*
> *Musical*
> *Absurdist/Surrealist*
> *Agitprop*
> *Expressionist*
> *Minimalist*
> *Music Hall*
> *Commedia dell'Arte*
> *Greek Tragedy*
> *Folk Play (mummers/medieval mystery play)*
> *Sitcom*
> *Children's Television*
> *Shakespeare*
> *Restoration*
> *Thunderbirds Puppets*
> *Star Wars*
> *Street, innit*

Now mix up the style cards and place them on the floor, spread out and face down, next to the playing space – but somewhere no one will slip over them!

Ask all the players to line up in pairs or small groups, ready to jump into the space. You then read out the first title and shout 'Go!' One of the players must pick up a style card and the group must play the titled section of the play in the style dictated by the card. As soon as they finish their section, they must run to the back of the line, you read out title number two, they pick a style card at random, and play continues.

The Aim of the Game

This is a fun and fast-paced way to explore modes of performance with a sense of spontaneity and imagination. By picking cards at random there is no temptation to match style with appropriate sections, meaning that the results are often original and unexpected. If you prefer, you could ask players to match styles with sections in order to create a specific interpretation of their story.

In terms of devising, this game allows you to think outside the proverbial box in terms of mode of performance, and to question whether our initial instincts (usually towards naturalism) are necessarily the most dramatically effective. It can seem scary to impose a performance style on what might well be a serious piece, but sometimes the most effective way of dealing with an emotional moment on stage can be something more representational or abstract.

+ Blank prompt cards, pens	
Players	**Skills**
8+	Improvisation, Imagination, Focus, Characterisation

Match Point

A game that tests the 'less is more' theory, in which you have to tell your story concisely before the flame goes out.

How to Play

Note: This game requires responsible, mature players.

This game was used by John Arden at the Royal Court Theatre to teach young writers the advantages of a minimalist approach.

Ask players to sit in a circle. They are going to be asked, one by one, to introduce themselves and tell everyone their life story. However, they only have from the moment their neighbour lights the match until the flame dies. As soon as the light is extinguished, they must finish.

Undoubtedly the first player will attempt to give as much information as humanly possible within the short space of time, rushing through information and boring the other players. This may well happen for the first few players. However (and you can choose whether to suggest this or not), as you go around the group, they will begin to realise that being bombarded with information is not interesting, and will (hopefully) think a little more cleverly about the content.

Ultimately, the most effective responses are often just a couple of select words. The players should observe how, in a certain space of time, we can communicate in an engaging manner. It is far more interesting to hear one unusual thing about someone than hear an entire garbled family history. It is often engaging to see how the players try different ideas in order to capture their audience. Some of the best responses I have seen have involved a single word or phrase and then the player has blown out the flame themselves!

The Aim of the Game

This is a simple but effective way of exploring narrative, storytelling and communication methods. It encourages players to think carefully about vocabulary and quantity of information. Relate this to the importance and dangers of exposition in terms of narrative technique.

Variations and Extensions

You can also use this method for exploring other stories. Whilst devising a piece based on myths and legends at East 15 Drama School, I asked each player to relate a story from their research of local myths in the time before the flame died. Initially they told their stories at high speed, incorporating as much information as possible, communicating very little. However, when given a second chance, reflecting on their techniques, they took the opportunity to use other voices – to tell the story in the first person; to take on a character; to play with the order of the story; to deliver it in the dark so that only their mouths could be seen by the light of the flame; or to reveal the story as a conversation. The playfulness that developed from this simple exercise was exciting and certainly influenced the final piece.

+ Box of matches, sand for spent matches

Players	Skills
4+	*Storytelling, Succinctness, Analysis, Timing*

Convention Conundrum

30

A game that allows you to impose dramatic conventions on a scene.

How to Play

Either use a pre-existing scene from your devising ideas, or pick a simple scenario (perhaps a location or situation, like a railway platform, a soup kitchen or Ladies' Day at Ascot).

Firstly, talk with the actors about dramatic conventions and how theatre-makers use them to add interest and drama to a scene. Brainstorm a list of conventions; anything goes here, whether you think it could work for your scene or not. Here are some to get the group started:

> *Tableaux (freeze-frames)*
> *Split-screen (two simultaneous scenes)*
> *Soliloquy or monologue*
> *Mime*
> *Group silence*
> *Group reaction*
> *Choral speaking*
> *Direct address*

There are two ways to play this game. You could ask the actors to run the scene and then shout '*Stop!*' at any point. At this point, they have to come and pick one convention off the list (either at random or allow them to choose a suitable one) and then use it in the scene.

Alternatively, you can ask them to pick a certain number of conventions off the list at the beginning of the exercise, then give them ten minutes to incorporate them into the scene, before showing it. This is likely to stimulate more honed responses, as the group will choose conventions which best suit the piece. However, the spontaneity of the first mode of play helps to provoke unusual responses, which you could only dream up when reacting in the moment, on your feet. It is the unlikely pairings of these responses that often engender the best outcomes. For example, if you had a single character on stage and they were given 'split-screen' (where two pieces of action happen simultaneously), they would have to respond to this demand, perhaps by incorporating a second actor, so that we see two sides of the one personality being played out at once. They would have been unlikely to pick this convention if given the choice, but the randomness of selection here allows unusual and interesting outcomes to emerge.

The Aim of the Game

This game encourages a group to think about methods of storytelling, and to consider a range of dramatic forms in their performance, rather than sticking to the safest and simplest options.

Players	Skills
Any	*Ensemble Work,*
number	*Imagination, Spontaneity*

Stan's Game

A game that helps to clarify the shape and dynamics of the piece.

How to Play

Stanislavsky, the Father of Naturalism, used the principle of 'units' to establish the shape of the drama in any given scene. A unit is any one self-contained idea or eventuality in a scene. Every time there is a significant change of subject or activity, a new unit begins. Each unit is given a title which states, in simple terms, exactly what happens in it. It is important not to colour the title with interpretative values; they must be simple and neutral in order to allow us to explore their dynamics. A proposal scene might, for example, be comprised of five units:

    a.   Harry greets Rebecca

    b.   Rebecca suggests a stroll along the river

    c.   Harry and Rebecca talk about how they met

    d.   Harry proposes to Rebecca

    e.   Rebecca accepts

Some of these units might be a line long, others half a page. You can see that these unit titles give us little idea about the tone, dynamics or details of the scene – it is left up to us to imagine how this scene might play out.

Work together to unit your text. Read the text out loud. Every time an actor feels their line initiates a new idea, draw a line under the previous unit to mark the point of change clearly, then number and title the unit. Once you have worked through the whole scene, write the numbers and titles out on large pieces of paper and stick them to the wall. You now have an action-based map of the text.

Place the actors in their positions for the beginning of the scene but ask them to put their scripts down. Choose a narrator to read the unit titles. The narrator must read the titles boldly, as if he or she is the storyteller; the actors then respond by improvising to the titles. Choose whether or not you will allow them to use words; if so, a line or two is usually sufficient.

The aim is to play the contrasts and thought changes between units as vigorously as possible throughout this reduced version of the original play, in order to clearly reveal the dynamic shifts. Work through the play like this, improvising each scene quickly and energetically, led by the narrator.

The Aim of the Game

This game is a simple means of clarifying the action, gaining an overview of the shape of the play and highlighting the shifting dynamics. Often identifying these shifts can have a profound effect when returning to the text, ensuring the actors have the confidence to play each tonal change bravely. It is also an engaging way of plotting the emotional journey for individuals and ensuring the company is familiar with the narrative as a whole.

+ Script, large pieces of paper, pens	
Players	**Skills**
Any number	Characterisation, Analysis, Storytelling

Sir Anthony!

A fast-paced warm-up game that also investigates status.

How to Play

This game is based on my favourite game, *King of the Jungle*, and was developed in rehearsals for *The Rivals* as we wanted our warm-ups to be specific to the play. You can easily adapt this game to your own narrative.

Begin by talking about the status of the characters in the play – what defines that status, how does it change, who is dominant, who is subservient? Often there are several different types of status at play – a social status, an importance status, a knowledge-based status. In *The Rivals*, for example, the order of social status is almost directly in opposition with the order of who knows the most – some of the servants, as in many period comedies, have more inside knowledge and wit than their masters.

Choose which type of status ranking you are going to use – social status is the easiest, but you could use knowledge, power or age. Ask the actors to line up in order of where they think they are in the ranking. This will undoubtedly warrant some interesting discussions, which you can return to later. Move into a circle with a chair placed behind the highest-status character, to mark where the order begins. Ask each actor to invent a simple gesture for their character. Go around the circle one by one and ask each actor to teach their gesture to the group, saying their character name as they do their gesture. The trick is to remember both the gesture for each character, and the order around the circle. Simple gestures are best, and for *The Rivals* ours were as follows:

> SIR ANTHONY – *Two arms flung forward, fists out*
>
> JACK – *Facing sideways, one fist towards the forehead, the other behind the back*
>
> LYDIA – *Arms up emphatically*
>
> JULIA – *A coy curtsy*
>
> FAULKLAND – *A melancholic palm to forehead*
>
> SIR LUCIUS – *Hand as a gun pointing towards the next person*

MRS MALAPROP – *A comic curtsy*

BOB ACRES – *A weakling fist shaken in the air*

FAG – *Touching the nose in a knowing way*

DAVID – *The doffing of an imaginary cap*

LUCY – *Sneakily patting the back pocket*

THOMAS – *A humble bow*

Sir Anthony (or your highest-status equivalent) always begins. Robin, who plays Sir Anthony, performs his gesture, throwing his firsts forward and saying '*Sir Anthony!*', before choosing another character; he spots Cian (who plays David), and says immediately '*David!*', doffing his imagined cap as he does. Cian then responds with his own name and gesture, then another's – '*David!*' (doffing his cap), '*Julia!*' (curtsying). Ella, who plays Julia, then must continue without hesitating. If she is too slow or makes a mistake (calls someone the wrong name, or gives the wrong gesture), she then moves down and becomes the lowest-status person in the circle. Everyone then moves up one to fill the spaces up to her position (those between her and Sir Anthony are safe as they don't have to move). This of course adds a challenge as the actors who have changed position now take on the name and gesture of the character one place up from them.

When the circle has moved around accordingly, Sir Anthony can begin again. Robin begins, with the appropriate gestures: '*Sir Anthony! Lucy!*' Lucy continues '*Lucy! Faulkland!*', and so on.

The aim is to be quick and energetic; daily play improves skills dramatically here! Ultimately, the objective is to 'become' Sir Anthony, and then maintain that position.

The Aim of the Game

This game is hilarious and a wonderful bonding experience. It is also quick and easy to play at the beginning of a rehearsal or before going on stage.

Players	Skills
6 +	*Focus, Speed, Confidence, Energy, Memory, Awareness*

Animal Instincts

A game that encourages actors to explore characters by using animal traits, instincts and mannerisms.

How to Play

Place three chairs to act as 'a bus stop', and ask the players to sit, as 'an audience', facing them. Ask for a volunteer, let's say Ben. Ben picks a slip of paper with an animal name written on it. He must now act as a human at the bus stop, but with the characteristics of the animal he chose. In this instance he was given a *fox*. He sidles to the bus stop, looking around suspiciously, then balances delicately on the edge of the chair.

Ask for a second volunteer. Dave volunteers and picks a *bear*. He moves heavily towards the bus stop, with a stooped physicality as if tired after a long day. He sits solidly on the chair, whilst Ben watches him warily.

The two actors must interact in a manner which befits their animal choices, but remembering throughout that they are not playing the animals, merely humans with the nuances of the creatures. Ben stealthily waits until Dave is looking the other way for the bus, before he cunningly picks his pocket. Dave feels this and suddenly towers above the cowering Ben, berating him from his full height and demanding his wallet back.

At an appropriate moment, ask for another volunteer. George goes in – he has chosen a *parrot*, so he struts in and immediately begins chatting away inappropriately. Ben, being the person who has been in for the longest, must then find a reason to leave the scene. With George chattering away, he easily finds an excuse and slinks foxily back to the audience. Continue the game, adding in new characters each round.

Once everyone has had a go, you may wish to extend the improvisation and perhaps redistribute animals for a group scene – rush hour at the station, a night at a local hotspot or a chaotic scene in an airport terminal. Encourage the actors to find a subtle balance between animalistic nuances and human traits.

If your devised piece has characters already, ask the actors to decide which animal is closest to their character, and to work on improvisations around their story, using their animal characteristics to underpin their interpretation. Remind them that speed, posture, movement, face, gesture and voice should all be considered, as well as temperament.

The Aim of the Game

The aim is to use animals as a way to explore character further, either in order to develop characters within the devised piece, or to create new characters from scratch. Primarily it is a tool to explore the multiplicity of any one character – face, body, voice and attitudes.

+ Animal names written on slips of paper	
Players	**Skills**
6+	Physicality, Characterisation, Analysis, Imagination

Humour Quad

A game that uses the ancient idea of the 'humours' as a means towards developing contrasting characters.

How to Play

Begin by investigating the concept and history of 'humourism'. The Ancient Greeks and Romans believed the human body was made up of four basic substances, the respective quantities and qualities of which determined an individual's health and character. This theory was later adopted by Islamic physicians and Europeans, before the advent of modern medicine. Personality, they believed, was characterised by whichever of these four liquid humours was most dominant. The four humours had the following qualities:

Humour	Colour	Quality	Personality Type	Characteristics
Yellow bile	Yellow	Choleric	Idealist	Short-tempered, driven, easily angered, irrational
Black bile	Black	Melancholic	Guardian	Sleepless, irritable, downcast, pessimist
Blood	Red	Sanguine	Artisan	Stubborn, courageous, optimist, amorous
Phlegm	White	Phlegmatic	Rational	Calm, unemotional, detached, cold

Mark out a cross on the floor to split the space into four quarters. Mark a coloured spot in each quarter, one red, black, yellow and white, to represent each humour. Now invite an actor, in neutral, to stand in each of the corners. As they enter the square they must adopt the characteristics of that humour.

Ask them to begin in the four far corners; this point is the purest of each humour as it is furthest away from any of the other squares. Ask the rest of the actors to watch and observe the physical manifestation of each humour. Next, ask the actors to take a step in a new direction into their square. They will inevitably move closer to one of the other humours. As they do so they must begin to let this new humour affect their personality, just subtly at this stage. Ask the actors to move one step at a time around their square, marking the minor changes in physicality and personality as they gain proximity to the other squares. Allow them to cross over into a new square, shifting personality to allow this new humour to dominate. Continue in this vein, allowing the actors to explore all four humours.

You can try this exercise with the characters from your devised play. Actors should stay in character, remaining true to the given persona, yet allow the mood, energy and tensions of the humours to affect physicality and emotion as they move between them.

It might be interesting to consider how each character would have been analysed according to this ancient system. What would their dominant humour have been? Which would be second? In order to find contrasting tones it is useful to ensure you have a variety of dominant humours across the personas in your play, to avoid overly similar characters.

The Aim of the Game

This game enables the company to gain new perspectives on established characters. By looking at humours we avoid the trap of playing two-dimensional stereotypes, as this exercise encourages actors to explore different dominant characteristics within their character's personality, varying their levels of energy, optimism and passion.

+ Tape, cones or markers	
Players	**Skills**
Any number	Improvisation, Characterisation

EXPLORATION

Rewind

A game in which the chronology of the play and the lead-up to each scene is investigated.

How to Play

This game is most effective when you have an outline of your narrative formed. However, you can also do it as an improvisation exercise using a famous story, as a fun way to investigate the art of storytelling.

Ask the actors to start at the beginning of their story, acting out the scene in its current form. When they start they must state the day and time of day. For example, whilst devising *Mad Kings and Englishmen*, a playful jaunt through English history, we looked at the life of Shakespeare. The most obvious option is to create a scene in which we see Will writing one of his most famous plays. Tom, our actor, announces that it is 5 p.m. on 1st May 1584. Then he sits centre stage as Will Shakespeare, quill in hand, writing frantically. The other actors watch from the sidelines.

At any point, one of the watching actors can shout *'Rewind!'* followed by a time and date. At this point, the performers on stage must stand up, turn around and cut to that particular moment. Other actors are free to join in as they see appropriate opportunities.

For example, Jo shouts *'Rewind, 4:45 p.m., the same day'* (fifteen minutes earlier). Tom jumps up, resumes his seat and this time sits staring blankly into space, painfully devoid of inspiration. We as an audience know that something now needs to happen to inspire him to write vigorously, as we saw him doing at 5 p.m. Harriet, therefore, jumps up, knocks on an imaginary door and says *'Hey Will, I got this love note from a boy called Romeo. What should I do?'* After handing out some friendly advice to Harriet's character, we then see Shakespeare make the connection and begin to write, thereby justifying the action of the later scene. Next, James, who is watching, shouts *'Rewind, 1st May 1564'* (twenty years earlier). Tom jumps up, turns around, Harriet re-enters and the two of them begin playing hopscotch as if they were at school. Then Charlie joins in, swaggering across the playground as the teenage Shakespeare's arch rival, Chris Marlowe. The game continues as the actors improvise in response to each new date.

There is no reason, of course, why you can't add fast-forwards too, if you want to explore the future consequences of events.

The Aim of the Game

The aim is two-fold. Firstly, it allows actors to further explore characters by creating a physicalised backstory. This encourages an investigation of the narrative in greater detail.

Secondly, it is a good way of generating new material. You may find that the scenes you create are more original and engaging than your original choices. Certainly a scene of Shakespeare and Marlowe having a teenage battle over a girl is a more amusing scenario than seeing the older Shakespeare sitting alone, writing. (This playground scene, incidentally, made it into the final play.)

EXPLORATION

Players	Skills
Any number	Storytelling, Improvisation, Imagination, Spontaneity, Ensemble Work

Role Reversal

An improvisation exercise in which we look at the given circumstances of a scene and play against them.

How to Play

For this exercise, you can either use a narrative you are working on, or a story that everyone knows. Split the group in two – a performing group and an audience.

Give the groups a short time (ten minutes is ideal) to create a four-minute version of their story, deciding who is playing who and what the key events are (beginning, middle and end). Ask them to have a practice run once through.

Once they have done so, pick a group to go first and hand out the SWAP cards to the audience (a card with the word 'SWAP' written on it). Ask the group to begin their performance.

At any point, an audience member can raise their SWAP card, shouting *'Stop! Swap!'* At this point the actors must freeze and the audience member suggests a reversal of something in the scene, in one of the following categories. Let's use Red Riding Hood as an example:

a) An *activity* swap: e.g. Red Riding Hood now gets into bed and the Wolf visits her.

b) A *character* swap: e.g. Red Riding Hood becomes the mean brute and the Wolf is the innocent.

c) A *location* swap: e.g. The bed is in the forest or the scene takes place at a different location entirely.

The Aim of the Game

This game encourages the group to move away from the most obvious choices whilst devising.

+ 'SWAP' cards	
Players	**Skills**
8+	*Improvisation, Spontaneity, Characterisation, Storytelling*

STAGE FOUR

DISTILLATION

Having completed the Exploration phase, the company will hopefully now have a clear sense of the piece. It will only be an outline, but the plot, characters and style should slowly be emerging. You will have generated a great deal of material, undoubtedly too much, and it will need honing and editing to form the final production.

Stage Four: Distillation is in some senses the most challenging as it involves throwing away ideas that actors will inevitably have become attached to.

It is often referred to as 'killing babies', which, whilst it sounds overdramatic, reflects the undeniably traumatic point when we are forced to make strong editorial decisions in order to form a clear, cohesive piece. Inevitably there will be disagreements about what is essential, sometimes driven by a worry about the size of an actor's part, rather than what is best for the piece as a whole. Ultimately, ego has to be put aside as you must choose the ideas that best serve the play. This is the most critical stage of devising as it determines the clarity and quality of the final work.

It is not, however, just about editing down and throwing away. This stage should be fun and generative as you play around with the material, asking questions about the focus, style and details of the piece. It is also a great opportunity to look critically at the piece and ensure that you have made the most imaginative choices. Finally, in this phase the actors are encouraged to find the detail in their performances.

Games like *Noises Off*, *Finding Alice*, *Seanchaí* and *The Dramagraph* investigate the narrative arc and style of storytelling. Meanwhile, *Gas Ring* and *Deconstruction* explore methods for adding dramatic weight to the story. As the final piece gains form and detail, *Statue of Liberty* and *Act Without Words* give the actors an opportunity to perform their texts without the restraints of holding a script, whilst *The Gallery Game* finds detail within the lines. *Where Am I?* considers the actors' relationship with the audience and reminds them to make the performance specific to the given performance space.

Noises Off

An investigation of the scenes between the scenes – a way to develop your narrative by looking at what happens 'offstage'.

How to Play

This exercise looks at how offstage events impact on characters' journeys, by playing them out as improvisations.

Ask the players to consider the structure of the narrative that has been created. Take a large piece of paper and plot the action on a timeline in one colour, clarifying when and where each scene or significant point of action takes place. Even if your play is abstract or non-linear, for the purposes of the exercise see if you can structure it on the paper to look at how each episode affects the next.

In a different coloured pen, write the key events that happen between the scenes. You might find that some of the most dramatic events happen offstage. The Ancient Greeks believed that it was more dramatic to imagine the moments of horror in a tragedy than to attempt to stage them. Events like murders were described but not seen. Sometimes a frozen image of the action would be shown; the actors would create a tableaux on a cart called an *ekkyklema*, which would be revealed at key moments. This way the audience understood the story clearly, but were left to imagine the full extent of the horrors – listening to the words to create their own mental pictures.

You should now have a list of key offstage events written down on the paper. Clear the space, ready for action, and pick up the dialogue at the climax of the first scene. When the scene ends, the actors must improvise the key events that happen next (using the timeline). If you can, try and make a link between the scenes; run straight from Scene One, into the improvisation, then into Scene Two.

You can repeat this exercise to explore all the unseen action. Often improvising what happens to a character just before their entrance helps to inform the energy and dynamics of their performance. To give an example, in Tom Stoppard's *The Real Thing*,

Max confronts his wife Annie about having an affair, having found an incriminating handkerchief in their car. Stoppard writes the scene of the confrontation with Annie, but we are left to imagine Max's discovery. An improvisation of the incident – when he finds the handkerchief, his immediate reaction and the realisation of his wife's infidelity – will inform his performance in the confrontation, and give him a greater grasp of his emotional journey. What has happened since the discovery? He has gone home, waited for Annie, run through whether to confront her or not, then she arrives… By playing the intervening action we see why Max has no choice but to confront his wife.

The Aim of the Game

Primarily, this exercise is a way to explore each character's journey, and to solidify the narrative of your devised piece. However, you may find the scenes you generate are worth adding to your production, or, as occasionally happens, are more dramatic than your current material, and so could replace other scenes.

+ Large pieces of paper, pens	
Players	**Skills**
6+	*Imagination, Storytelling, Characterisation*

Finding Alice

A game in which players retell the story, each time changing the order, to investigate structure, narrative arc and tension.

How to Play

Begin by splitting the narrative of your devised piece into five key units of action (usually the beginning, the event that changes the scenario, the crisis, the build towards the climax and the final denouement). Write a one-line summary or title for each unit, each one on a new piece of paper. Let's take the devised play *Finding Alice* by Ben Harrison as an example. The plot, greatly simplified, is as follows:

1) Miriam falls asleep in bed whilst reading *Alice in Wonderland* and wakes up in Wonderland.

2) The Queen of Hearts catches her with 'the book', which is banned in Wonderland! She tears the book up in a rage.

3) Miriam needs to read the end of the book to find out how to get home. She despairs!

4) She travels Wonderland finding the pages and piecing the book back together, before…

5) Arriving home, safe and sound.

Once you have titled the sections, perform a one-minute version of each section, playing them out chronologically.

Now comes the fun part. It is all too easy to choose a straightforward, chronological structure for a devised play. Often this will be the best option, in terms of clarity and narrative arc, but you may find a more unusual order suits your play better.

Try the following exercises. Firstly, put your five pieces of paper into a hat. The actors must pick them out in a random order and perform their one-minute scenes in this sequence.

Next, run them backwards, from five to one. Look at the way that the sources of tension and interest change when we focus on how an event happened rather that what happens next.

Finally, ask the actors to put the five scenes in order of importance. Try this sequence both in ascending and descending order of importance. How do the stakes change?

The Aim of the Game

This game encourages actors to experiment with structure. You may well decide that a chronological approach serves the play best. However, it is interesting to use this exercise to explore the way in which we invest in stories; is it how, why or what happens that arouses our curiosity and emotional investment the most?

+ Pens, paper, hat	
Players	**Skills**
Any number	Imagination, Storytelling, Characterisation

Gas Ring

A game in which players raise the stakes in a scene, 'turning up the heat' to add drama.

How to Play

You can apply the following exercise to any scene in your devised play. Whilst constructing their scenes, the group must always ask – what is at stake? What matters? What could go wrong? If there is nothing at risk then the scene will never take off.

Think about some of the most dramatic scenes in theatre. Memorable drama arises from the potential an event has to change the course of the characters' future. In Chekhov's *The Cherry Orchard*, we see Lopakhin building up the courage to ask Varya to marry him. Whilst marriage scenes are not unusual, this has particular dramatic resonance because Chekhov raises the stakes – everything relies on this proposal. For Varya it is not just her only likely chance of marriage, prosperity and security, but, more importantly, her one opportunity to secure her whole family's estate, their livelihoods and their beloved cherry orchard. The future of the whole family rests on whether or not Lopakhin can dispel his nerves and ask her. Chekhov expertly provides a dramatic denouement in this one moment, by setting the futures of all the characters in the balance.

So, consider what is at stake in every scene in your play. Arrange the stage so that you can play the scene out as usual. Ask everyone else to sit as a watching audience. As the scene progresses, the audience must look for points of interest. At any point they are allowed to shout out '*Stop! Raise the stakes!*', then identify the point that the actors should rewind to. The actors must then perform that part of the scene again, but find some way to increase the risk.

To give a simple example, Lorna visits Al's house. He offers her a cup of tea.

> LORNA: No, thank you, Alistair, I don't much like tea.
>
> AL: Oh well, what a shame.

LISA (*from the audience*): Stop! Raise the stakes,
'No, thank you, Alistair.'

LORNA: No, thank you, Alistair. I don't want tea
from you.

AL: Well, that's interesting, coming from a snob
like you! What's wrong with my tea!

They begin to argue but Lisa thinks the situation
could be even more dramatic.

LISA (*from the audience*): Stop! Raise the stakes,
'Well, that's interesting.'

AL: Well, that's interesting, coming from a
cheating wife like you!

LORNA: How dare you, I'd never accept tea
from you, you've probably poisoned it!

AL: Well, darling, you should have thought of that
before you ate that cucumber sandwich. Any
second now…

LORNA: Oh dear, oh no! I'm dying, help! Help!
I've been poisoned!

Lorna and Al thought quickly on their feet to raise
the level of risk in this scenario. Whilst this is a
comic example, if you choose subtle shifts in levels
you can often uncover simple ways to 'turn up the
heat'. Has it been a week, a month or a year since
this estranged couple saw each other? Did she
come round to borrow milk, to get divorce papers
signed or to deliver some terrible news? What
could add pressure to the characters, in order to
amplify their emotional levels?

The Aim of the Game

This game aims to raise the actors' awareness of
what is at risk in the scene and thereby to play the
tension dramatically. It is also an opportunity to add
to your devised drama by increasing the emotional
intensity, changing the narrative to add to the
pressure cooker.

Players	Skills
Any number	Improvisation, Imagination, Characterisation, Analysis

Statue of Liberty

A method of liberating the actors to play with the text freely before they have learnt it.

How to Play

Do this exercise when the script is written but before the actors have learnt it.

Designate each actor a 'reader' who isn't in that scene. The readers must stand either just behind their actor, or at the edge of the space near the actor.

The readers must quietly whisper to the actor each of his or her lines, without any interpretation or emotion, as neutrally as possible. The actor then repeats the line, but with full emotion and using the space freely. Encourage the actors to be as active and imaginative as possible, enjoying the liberty of working without a script in hand.

It is important that the readers feed lines of a length that can be repeated easily; they should break up long passages, otherwise actors will concentrate on remembering the phrase rather than on engaging with the feelings.

This exercise dispels the problem of static performance that inevitably descends when actors have scripts in hand. By simply listening to the fed lines, the actor can enjoy the mental and physical freedom to explore the script fully.

This exercise works equally well with monologues.

The Aim of the Game

The aim is to free the actors up interpretatively, allowing them to hear the words as if for the first time and to deliver them with as much energy and originality as possible.

+ One copy of the script	
Players	**Skills**
2+	*Imagination, Physicality, Characterisation*

Seanchaí

A storytelling game in which the speaker retells the tale in one of many narrative styles.

How to Play

A seanchaí was an Irish storyteller who travelled from village to village telling tales in exchange for board and lodgings. Their trade was storytelling so they were experts in their craft, keeping their audience rapt with every word. In this game, write the names of different storytelling styles on paper and put them into a hat:

A seanchaí storytelling
A news broadcast
A eulogy
A best man's speech
Teenage gossip behind the bike-sheds
A bedtime story
An academic lecture
A witness on the stand
A deathbed reminiscence
A critic's report
A watercooler moment

Players must take it in turns to tell the narrative of the play to the group, who must then guess the style. You could choose modes of delivery that specifically relate to your play. Work with a time limit on each retelling, or divide the story up so as not to be repetitive.

Try and find the different colours throughout the story. Work on modulation specifically – variety of pitch, intonation, pace, tone colour and volume.

The Aim of the Game

This game reinforces the actors' familiarity with the plot. It also allows them to focus on the dynamics, to identify peaks and troughs, and to pinpoint the emotional shifts.

+ Pens, paper, hat	
Players	**Skills**
6+	Storytelling, Characterisation, Succinctness

Deconstruction

An exercise that enables actors to create new scripts from familiar texts.

How to Play

Give out the original texts – you can either use a text the group has written or use a new one. Poetry works particularly well for this exercise, particularly emotive and visually engaging poems such as those by Pablo Neruda and Maya Angelou. Share the text you have chosen with the group, asking someone to read it out, so that you are all familiar with it in its original form.

Divide the players into smaller groups of between two and five players. Designate each small group as either an A, B or C group; the letters denote three textual approaches so ensure you have at least one group of each type.

Approach A: Text

> This approach is the simplest of the three. This group works on a performance that honours the original text exactly. They must perform the words in the most interesting way possible, paying close attention to imagery, character and dynamics, and creating a physical response to any images in the text. Dialogue should be spoken in character; modulation (variation of pitch, tone, pace, volume and dynamics) should be used to create an engaging aural response. Varying the number of speakers will help to emphasise key moments. The task is to lift the text off the page.

Approach B: Half-text

> Often we engage more with what isn't being said than what is. '*Do you fancy a…*' is a much more interesting proposition than '*Do you fancy a cheese sandwich?*'; the second leaves no mystery and no room for drama. This group's first task, therefore, is to read the text out leaving the last word off every phrase. Once they have tried this, repeat the exercise but this time the group stops halfway through each phrase. The third exercise pushes this reduction even further – only deliver the first word of

each phrase. See which of these three exercises provides the most rich and engaging response. The group then works out a short performance of the text using this technique. They can use all three forms of reduction at some point during the text, or stick to whichever they feel gave the most effective reading. As Beckett famously proposed, you will undoubtedly find that less is often more.

Approach C: Subtext

This group must look at the text as if there are two layers – the immediate meaning of the lines, and then the subtext implied underneath. Using the written text as the surface text, write out what you think the subtext might be underneath each line. What is the writer really suggesting? What is the character actually saying? Try and capture any nuances and changes of tone as accurately as possible. Then work out a short performance using the subtext script instead of the original text.

Having given everyone adequate time to prepare, ask each group to share their pieces. They will undoubtedly be surprised by the contrasts, considering they are derived from the same source text. This could initiate a discussion of subtext and the dramatic concepts of reduction and minimalism, as employed by Beckett. You could look at his short play *Breathe* as an example of the 'less is more' principle in action.

The Aim of the Game

This exercise gives players the tools to deconstruct one text and form another from it. It dispels the myth of the text as sacred, encouraging us to pull it apart and to recreate it without inhibitions. It should also demonstrate that there is no one 'correct' way to work with text.

+ A written text	
Players	**Skills**
6+	*Analysis, Storytelling, Characterisation, Writing*

Where Am I?

A game that investigates the effect of the theatre space on performance.

How to Play

Write the following headings on separate cards and place them into the hat:

> *17,000 Greek Amphitheatre (Greek tragedy)*
>
> *4,000 Drury Lane (Restoration comedy)*
>
> *1,800 Shakespeare's Globe (twenty-first century)*
>
> *800 West End Theatre (Victorian melodrama)*
>
> *500 Regional Theatre (e.g. Exeter Northcott, Salisbury Theatre)*
>
> *100 A hay cart in an Italian Piazza (Commedia dell'Arte)*
>
> *50 Studio Theatre (Realism)*
>
> *1 Television Acting*

Split the group into pairs or small groups according to your text, so that actors are working with others they have scenes with, if possible. Each subgroup should pick one of the cards out of the hat. They must rehearse their scene as if they are performing in the venue and to the audience capacity written on the card, varying their manner of audience address, size and style of acting accordingly. For example, the Greek amphitheatre requires a declamatory, gesture-filled style, played upwards and outwards. In contrast, the hay cart requires a highly physical, energetic style, directly addressing the audience in order to keep the bustling crowd engaged. The television actor, in contrast, should perform as though they are alone in the room. For West End or regional theatre, think about upholding the convention of the 'fourth wall'. For the Globe, remember to play to an audience you can see, from the highest balconies ('the gods') to the groundlings in the yard.

Each group should then perform their scene to the group, who must guess where they are, the capacity of the space and the style of acting. If you wish you can add other cards to give a wider variety of performance styles.

The Aim of the Game

This game encourages actors to be aware of their relationship with the audience. It is particularly useful for rehearsing plays that require direct address – Restoration and Georgian comedies, for example – or if you are performing in an unusual venue. I used it when rehearsing Nell Leyshon's play *Bedlam* for Shakespeare's Globe, as this space demands an energetic relationship between actor and audience. I also used it when rehearsing Hannah Cowley's eighteenth-century comedy *The Belle's Stratagem* in order to clarify where and when interaction is helpful, and to encourage the actors to be braver about engaging with the spectators.

+ Pens, cards, hat	
Players	**Skills**
6+	*Analysis, Characterisation, Awareness*

DISTILLATION

The Gallery Game

A game that investigates the text as if it was a visual landscape.

How to Play

Each actor chooses a scene or a speech to work on, and begins by reading through the text once. Every time they hit a concrete image – for example, an object, a person's name, a place – they should underline it.

Once they have done so, they return to the beginning of the text and, in a different colour, mark any abstract images – ideas, concepts, feelings.

Finally, they go through the text for a third time, and underline any descriptive language in another colour.

Next, ask them to take a walk around the room and imagine themselves in a space where all the ideas from the speech are visible. They could be in a gallery filled with paintings of these ideas, at a museum, out on a hilltop with a view of the panorama, in a village meeting – whatever is most appropriate for their speech. A gallery or museum works for any speech, the others are more specific.

Each actor finds a partner and speaks their text to them; every time they encounter an image, they show it to their partner, physically, in the room – pointing it out, using the expressive language to describe it. They should try and interest their partner in each individual image and moment. Once completed, they should consider the tempo of their journey. Which were the most exciting images? Which sections of the speech are a gentle meander and which are moments of desperation?

This exercise works as effectively for conversations as it does for speeches. In this instance, the characters speaking are both showing one another around. Often this becomes a battle between the pair to persuade the other that their ideas are more interesting to look at!

The Aim of the Game

By visualising the text, we can highlight the imagery and pay attention to the detail of the language. This exercise encourages actors to unpick the text, take note of the specific verbal choices and explore the rhythm and shape of their speeches.

It is particularly useful when an actor is faced with a lengthy monologue. In rehearsals for *Palace of the End* by Judith Thompson, which consists of three twenty-minute monologues about the Iraq War, I found it useful as a way to liberate the company from the convention of sitting still and plotting the changes of thought. After several days of 'round the table' work, it was immensely freeing to put the piece on its feet and to investigate the possibilities of who each character is talking to. This helped to clarify the actors' objectives and to find new interpretative ideas.

+ A written text, pens	
Players	**Skills**
Any number	Analysis, Storytelling, Characterisation, Writing

The Dramagraph

A game in which you visually identify the characters'
dramatic journeys – a giant dramagraph!

How to Play

In order for a narrative to be engaging, characters'
journeys must have an arc, a journey during which
their situation changes – this is the essence of
drama. The dramatic arc comprises of a character's
rise or fall, in terms of achieving happiness, for
example. Usually, a story will contain positive and
negative arcs, in order to give a sense of equilibrium
and contrast.

Take, for example, *Macbeth*. Macbeth himself
begins as a hero, rises to honour and ends as a
tyrant, and a dead one at that. His fatal flaw drives
him to destruction. His arc, if we drew it on a
graph, would begin at a midpoint, rise, and then fall
sharply.

Balanced with that, Macduff is a courageous man
who loses everything when Macbeth has his family
murdered. Eventually, he achieves his revenge and
kills Macbeth. His arc is in opposition with
Macbeth's; it begins at a midpoint, hits an ultimate
low and then rises again (although we suspect he
ends lower than he begins, as his wife and children
have been killed).

Within your devised piece, you should work
towards having a range of positive and negative arcs
across the characters – most will have a peak or a
trough at some point along the journey.

For each character, draw a simple line graph, with
the time frame of the play plotted along the
horinzontal axis, and a 'happiness-ometer' along the
vertical side.

Plot a dot for how happy they are at the beginning
of the play. To assess their level of happiness, it
helps to work out what their objective in life is, and
how close they are to reaching that goal.

Next, plot the final dot. Are they better or worse
off? Closer to their goal or farther from it? Then
plot the central points where this changes. There is
likely to be a main event that will trigger a change –

perhaps there are several. In as much detail as you can, mark the points of change throughout each character's journey.

The whole company should compare their graphs. Hopefully they will be contrasting. If you find all have a similar shape, consider whether it would give you a stronger narrative line to vary the journeys more.

You can plot all of the characters onto one giant graph now, using a different colour for each character. See what the final picture is and what this says about the devised play.

The Aim of the Game

This exercise allows the group to investigate and potentially reconsider the plot development through exploring each character's individual journey, and how that contributes to the whole.

+ Large pieces of paper, pens	
Players	**Skills**
Any number	Analysis, Storytelling, Characterisation, Writing

Act Without Words

One of the most valuable exercises in the book: performing a mimed version of the play.

How to Play

In this exercise the actors are required to strip back, putting words to one side and simply playing the action. They must communicate both the text and the subtext without words.

There are two ways to play this game, the first with actors reading; the second with no words at all.

In the first version, allocate each actor a spokesperson. The spokesperson stands on the sidelines and reads in the actor's lines. The actors stand in the space and perform the actions of the scene, thoughts and intentions, concentrating on physical detail and marking the minutiae of the scene, but without speaking. Work at a slower pace than usual, allowing the actors time to listen to each line and then respond.

In the alternative version, a silent exercise, the actors must perform the scene, playing each thought, idea and action without words. Wait until the actors know the text well before attempting this. They should take their time to work on the physical detail of their relationships – the proximity, the body language. Encourage them to perform with a heightened awareness of what they are doing in order to remember these discoveries when they return to the text later. You may well be surprised by how engaging these silent scenes can be.

The Aim of the Game

Physicality is often a secondary tool in the communication of a character, text being the primary. This exercise allows actors to focus on their physical personalities and relationships without having to worry about words. It can be a liberating experience.

Players	Skills
Any number	Physicality, Storytelling, Characterisation

STAGE FIVE

PRESENTATION

This is a truly exciting stage. Throughout the previous four phases, the company will have worked together to construct the play, investigating every aspect of character, theme, narrative and style. Soon, with any luck, the play will be ready to face an audience.

Stage Five: Presentation focuses the skills and tools needed to share the work with the audience, projecting and presenting the piece mentally, emotionally, audibly and physically. In this section you will find simple focus exercises like *Breath Control* and *Rain Tree*. *Ask the Audience* and *Grandmother's Gone* allow actors to find a deeper sense of focus and ensemble before going on stage. *Narrative Ring* asks the company to concentrate on the story they will be telling, to ensure they can deliver it with clarity and detail. The vocal exercises are self-explanatory, each designed to warm up different parts of the vocal equipment, and to engender a spirit of energy and concentration that will inform the performance.

Ensemble, finally, is an opportunity to revisit the very first starting point – at the beginning there was just the group, just the actors – no story, no characters, no play. Everyone has come a great distance in getting to this point, so enjoy the performance and remember that, just as a collaborative group formed the piece, collaboration must continue on stage. The best theatrical performances are always given with a sense of ensemble and sharing.

Breath Control

A range of breathing exercises to get the lungs working and the mind focused.

How to Play

Awareness of the Breath

Here are the instructions to give to the company, and which every actor should follow:

- Stand up straight, feet comfortably hip-width apart. Place your hands on your diaphragm. Breathe in, allowing the breath to fill the ribcage, moving it upwards and outwards. Ensure you are not raising your shoulders, as this means you are not breathing deeply into your body, but taking shallow breaths, only using the top of your lungs and creating unnecessary tension.

- Pay attention to the effect of the breath. Avoid tightening in the throat, and allow the air to expand the lungs (the ribs and belly should expand outwards as you breathe in, not, as some think, flatten and disappear).

- Stand with one hand gently around your throat and the other flat against the ribs in your back. Breathe in and, as you do, feel the ribcage expand upwards and outwards.

- Hold your arms out in front of you, palms facing each other, and pull the hands outwards to the side of the body, breathing in as you do. Allow the hands to move back to centre front as you breathe out.

- Move onto the floor. Position yourself on all fours, looking down into the floor and keeping your knees hip-width apart.

- Breathe in, again feeling the ribs expanding and allow the lungs and abdomen to fill with air, moving towards the floor. Push the air out more vigorously, allowing the muscles to move back in towards the spine as you exhale.

Be continually aware not to raise your shoulders, and allow yourself to relax as you do these exercises.

Eights

Stand in a circle. As a group, everyone must:

- Breathe in for eight (you should click your fingers eight times to guide the group).
- Hold the breath for eight (click eight times).
- Breathe out for eight (click eight times).

Repeat the breathing cycle, increasing the number of counts each time by two.

The Aim of the Game

These exercises are intended to focus the actors, in addition to bringing an awareness of correct breath control.

Players	Skills
Any number	*Breath Control, Focus, Voice Work*

Rain Tree

A vocal warm-up that encourages familiarity. It involves working in small groups to perform a physical and vocal warm-up on one player, the 'rain tree'.

How to Play

A note on the physical warm-up process: One effective method of waking up the body is to tap or slap your skin lightly to promote circulation and a feeling of liveliness. Think about the way you might slap your own face to wake yourself up when falling asleep. Many physical warm-ups incorporate gently tapping your skin all over. We often do this whilst humming to locate the placement of the sound and vibrations in the chest and resonating chambers. In this exercise, the other players perform this action on the person in the middle of the circle. Of course, this requires sensible participants and a level of both restraint and respect. It can be a highly effective warm-up with sensible players.

Split the group into teams of four or five players. One player stands in the middle of the group; they are the 'rain tree'. The others form a circle around the tree; they are the storm. They then perform the following sequence of movements and sounds on the rain tree, thus performing an energising vocal warm-up themselves, whilst the rain tree simultaneously receives a stimulating physical wake-up.

The players begin by emulating the lightest rain, building through heavier rain to a thunderstorm, and then fading to a pleasant day. Each sound should be performed with full use of lip and tongue muscles in order to prove an effective vocal warm-up. The different phases should be moved through naturally, with the players sensing when to make a transition, rather than talking about it. The rain tree stands upright with their eyes closed throughout.

> *Light rain* – Using the tips of their fingers only, players lightly touch the rain tree, moving their fingers softly all over (obviously within the realms of decency). The accompanying sound: *'Tic, tic, tic, tic.'*

Pattering rain – Players increase the frequency and weight of their finger touches. Sound: *'Pitter patter, pitter patter.'*

Droplets – Players gently touch the rain tree, allowing fingers to move outwards on contact, as if heavier drops are breaking on impact. Sound: *'Plop, plop, plop, plop.'*

Gushing rain – Players brush the rain tree in light downwards motions as if water is cascading down the bark. Sound: *'Shhh, shhh, shhh.'*

Storm – Players tap the tree all over, as one would in a vigorous massage, using both hands in quick succession to give the impression of a powerful shower of rain. Sound: Storm noises, using their full voices and moving through all pitches to exercise the voice fully.

Next, reverse the process so the storm slowly moves back through each phase until it passes. When you have completed a rain sequence from start to finish, one of the other players in the group becomes the rain tree. Repeat this until all participants have had a turn.

The Aim of the Game

This exercise simultaneously provides an effective vocal warm-up for the rain-makers and a physical warm-up for the rain tree. It also encourages familiarity.

Variations and Extensions

This game produces the natural evolution of a soundscape. Use this as a springboard for other work on creating sounds using voice and the human body. Whilst weather is an ideal place to start, you could look at a range of environments or locations as alternatives.

Players	**Skills**
4+	*Voice Work, Ensemble Work*

Ask the Audience

A game that creates a sense of ensemble and encourages choral performance.

How to Play

Split the group into two, one half (Group A) to *perform* as an audience, the others (Group B) to be the real audience. Ask Group A to arrange themselves in an audience configuration, either sitting in rows or standing up, facing Group B.

Group A must imagine they are watching a dramatic piece of theatre. They cannot discuss in advance the genre of the play, this must develop as their performance does. They must watch the imagined play intensely, reacting emotionally to what is going on in front of them on stage. Reactions can include laughter, fear at spooky moments, frustration or disgust, and joy at a happy event. The actors must react simultaneously, as a group, establishing where the moments of comedy or dread and so on are, without any one audience member leading the group. This requires a good deal of group focus, careful timing and ensemble playing.

Ask Group B to comment on what worked about the scene. You can also ask them if they spotted any leaders. If they did, give the group another go and see if they can work together as an ensemble more closely.

Then ask Group B to take the stage and repeat the exercise. If you want to put a contrasting slant on it, try asking them to be an audience at a tennis match, at the opera or at an arena watching gladiators – this will allow further opportunities for characterisation.

The Aim of the Game

This exercise demands a great deal of focus if it is to work effectively. It is a fun way to introduce choral performance. Try filming it to help the actors assess their own ensemble playing.

Players	Skills
10+	*Ensemble Work, Focus, Timing*

Grandmother's Gone

Based on the well-known children's favourite Grandmother's Footsteps, *the group must act as an ensemble to react to an imaginary grandmother.*

How to Play

In *Grandmother's Footsteps*, players move slowly and silently from one end of the room to the other, towards 'Grandmother', who has her back turned. Every time she turns around, the players must freeze. If she sees someone moving, she points at them and they must go back to the far end of the room. The aim is to touch Grandmother, and the first player to do so becomes Grandmother for the next round.

This version, however, is far more difficult, as there is no Grandmother! The group must act as an ensemble, creeping towards the imaginary Grandmother. They must then try and sense when they are all going to freeze, imagining that Grandmother has turned around. They must then all begin moving at the same time, continuing their course towards the invisible Grandmother. It may take several attempts to get the group working as a coordinated ensemble. Encourage the players to avoid leading as much as possible.

The Aim of the Game

The aim is to explore the sense of ensemble and to become more adept at working with awareness. It is a difficult skill to master. Inevitably there will be some leaders in the group who dictate when movement starts and stops. Try playing this at the beginning of every rehearsal; you are bound to notice the progress over time.

Players	Skills
6+	*Ensemble Work, Focus, Control*

Narrative Ring

A game that focuses on the performance ahead,
encouraging actors to think through the narrative.

How to Play

In this game the actors create several reduced
versions of the play to pinpoint the key events and
the characters' dramatic trajectories. Work through
this series of exercises, each of which requires a
different method of reduction.

Ask the players to form a circle. The first task is to
retell the story of the play in one rotation of the
circle. Each player gives one phrase that
summarises each stage in the story, finishing on '*and
then…*' to indicate where the next player should
begin. For example, Amy might start with: '*It was
Claire and Neal's wedding, and Neal was trying to find
the rings, and then…*' Wendy, Amy's immediate
neighbour, then continues the story: '*He
remembered he'd had them in his pocket when that
strange women had bumped into him, and then…*'
The aim is to get to the end of the story within one
round of the circle. For this to work, everyone
must be succinct, and must think as a team about
how much to tell. The group should be halfway
through the narrative when the story is halfway
around the circle. This is impossible if the initial
speakers get overenthusiastic!

Once the story has been told around the circle,
move on to the second challenge: to perform each
scene in a ten-second, reduced version (think of the
Reduced Shakespeare Company). If the play does
not have designated scenes, try dividing it in
another way – by key events, for example. The
group must stand up and perform a miniature
version of each scene lasting strictly no more than
ten seconds.

The third challenge, which is even trickier, is to
repeat this exercise but allow each actor to say only
one line. It does not need to be a line from the play;
they should improvise something that summarises
their role in the scene. To use our earlier example,
the actor playing Neal may jump in and say '*I can't
believe it, my rings have gone!*' Be strict about what

constitutes a line; six or seven phrases strung together with a series of 'ands' is cheating.

The fourth challenge is for every actor to jump in and give one line for their character for the whole play. This does not mean summarisang everything that happens to them in they play; more that they indicate their character by commenting on their journey or super-objective. Neal might therefore say *'If only I'd known about the curse, I'd have lost the rings earlier!'*

The final task is a group task – the group must summarise the whole play in a single phrase. Give them a minute or so to come up with the best line; it could be the moral of the story or a funny new title. They should see how inventive they can be.

The Aim of the Game

The aim of this game is primarily to focus the actors on the story they are telling. By plotting the narrative they will consider the moments to highlight, contemplate the arc of the story in terms of tension and momentum, and think about how their character fits into the play as a whole. It is a fun exercise in terms of deconstructing the story. It also ensures every performer feels like an integral part of the piece, no matter how small their role is.

Players	**Skills**
Any number	*Focus, Storytelling, Awareness, Memory, Ensemble Work, Succinctness*

Vocal Warm-Up 1:
Neither Up Nor Down

A warm-up exercise to coordinate voice and movement.

How to Play

Everyone stands in a circle, singing the nursery rhyme 'The Grand Old Duke of York' as a group, marching on the spot as they do it. The words are as follows:

Oh, the grand old Duke of York,
He had ten thousand men.
He marched them up to the top of the hill,
And he marched them down again.
And when they were up, they were up.
And when they were down, they were down.
And when they were neither halfway up,
They were neither up nor down.

Now repeat the song, making the following changes each time:

Round 1 – March round in a circle, singing whilst marching, but this time at the level of a stage whisper, articulating each line and stressing each consonant sound.

Round 2 – Still marching, every time the group gets to the word '*up*', they do not say it, but instead rise onto tiptoes, e.g. 'He marched them (rise) to the top of the hill.' Leave a pause where the word should have been.

Round 3 – Reinstate the word '*up*', and this time take out the word '*down*'. Each time the group gets to where the word '*down*' should be, they bend the knees in a squat, e.g. 'And he marched them (squat) again.'

Round 4 – Take out both the words '*up*' and '*down*', rising and squatting whilst marching, at the appropriate times.

Round 5 – The most challenging round! Take out all the words except the words '*up*' and '*down*'. After counting the group in, they march in silence until they get to the exact moment the first '*up*' is said. This is harder than it might sound, so everyone must listen carefully and speak the words in their heads as if they are saying them out loud.

Round 6 – Take out all the words. Just march and maintain the rises and squats for '*up*' and '*down*'. This forces everyone to concentrate on group timing.

Round 7 – For a bit of fun, try marching without words but beating the rhythm out in any way you like. Keep in the '*ups*' and '*downs*' to punctuate the rhythm. The actors can stamp or clap the rhythm, beat out the base beat or the rhythm of the words, thereby creating a sonorous rhythmic piece (or that's the hope, at least!).

The Aim of the Game

This is a good way to focus the group and build the spirit of an ensemble, whilst developing a collective sense of timing. Everyone needs to articulate carefully throughout, in order to get the benefits of this vocal exercise.

Players	**Skills**
Any number	*Voice Work, Projection, Breath Control, Focus, Articulation*

53 Vocal Warm-Up 2: Vowel Jazz

A physical and vocal exercise to warm up the voice.

How to Play

Everyone stands in a circle with their left foot in the middle. On your instruction, the group begin tapping out a regular beat on the floor by twisting the ankle left, right, left, right, and tapping the toe on the floor on each twist to set a 'one, two, one, two' beat.

Ask someone to begin, let's call her Carice. Carice chooses a consonant sound, 'B' for example. She says '*Ba!*' The group then begin the 'vowel jazz', as follows, using Carice's chosen consonant to begin each line, with the rhythm '*and 1, and 2, and 3*':

Ba ba, ba ba,
Bey bey, bey bey,
Bee bee, bee bee,
Bi bi, bi bi, (*Pronounced to rhyme with 'eye'.*)
Bo bo, bo bo,
Bu bu, bu bu. (*Pronounced to rhyme with 'you'.*)
(*Wait for four beats.*)

The feet keeping the rhythm move on every double sound, e.g.:

And 1	And 2	And 3	And 4	And 5	And 6
Tap	Tap	Tap	Tap	Tap	Tap
Left	Right	Left	Right	Left	Right
Ba ba	*Ba ba*	*Bey bey*	*Bey bey*	*Bee bee*	*Bee bee*

And 7	And 8	And 1	And 2	And 3	And 4
Tap	Tap	Tap	Tap	Tap	Tap
Left	Right	Left	Right	Left	Right
Bi bi	*Bi bi*	*Bo bo*	*Bo bo*	*Bu bu*	*Bu bu*

(*Wait 5, 6, 7, 8...*)

Next, it is the turn of the player on Carice's immediate right, in this case Ben, who chooses a new consonant and must begin without letting the rhythm falter after the end of Carice's round. He chooses 'Z' and says '*Za!*' Everyone then swaps their left foot with their right, and the exercise begins again on the other foot:

Za za, za, za,
Zey zey, zey zey (*etc.*)

Never stop the beat, continuing it on the same foot
until the new consonant is stated.

The Aim of the Game

This warm-up exercise cycles through the key
vowel sounds in order to warm up the voice, and
uses consonants to engage the facial muscles. The
trick is to coordinate voice and body, and to work
as a group to get the ensemble moving and
speaking as one. Be sure to enunciate throughout,
and remember to breathe properly in order to fully
support the voice.

Players	Skills
Any number	*Voice Work, Projection, Breath Control, Focus, Articulation*

Vocal Warm-Up 3: Tongue-Twisters

A selection of vocal warm-ups that work through a variety of vowel and consonant sounds.

How to Play

These are all short tongue-twisters that can either be sung to a basic tune on each note of the scale, or repeated in a spoken voice. Each focuses on a different speech sound, so try and run through a range of them in order to warm up the whole voice. It's a good idea to do a quick face massage first, working on loosening up the facial muscles.

1) She is the epitome of virile femininity.

2) Stella was an umbrella seller with a cellar.
   Said the fellahs, 'You're that cellar dweller Stella, you're that seller. Can I buy an umbrella?'
   That is what they'd tell our Stella, then Stella the umbrella cellar, she'd say 'No'.

3) Jon's swan sung a swansong on a silver pool at night, till a silver-sided sea bream sunk the swan right out of sight.

4) Popper, Topper, Copper Top.

5) A Panda called Miranda loved a bland man from Uganda,
   But the bland man from Uganda loved Amanda who was grander.

6) Max had a black mac
   In his black backpack,
   And some snacks,
   A stack of Snack-a-Jacks.

7) Freshly fried flying fish.
   What a wish for a fried fish dish.

8) Dunk the skunk had a run in with a punk,
   But the punk was drunk so Dunk dunked the drunk.

9) Potassium, Magnesium, Lithium and Selenium, Polonium and Sodium, Radon, Aluminium.

PRESENTATION

10) Pretty Kitty caught the kitten in the kitchen flap.

11) The sheik's sixth sheep's sick.

12) Seventy-seven benevolent elephants.

13) Freddie Thrush flies through thick fog fast.

14) A critical cricket critic critiques.

15) Unique New York, New York unique.

The Aim of the Game

These are quick vocal warm-ups to ensure the voice is ready for performance, to work the facial muscles and to focus the mind.

Players	Skills
Any number	*Voice Work, Projection, Breath Control, Focus, Articulation*

Vocal Warm-Up 4: Trinidada

A tongue-twisting warm-up that involves some tricky challenges of articulation.

How to Play

Everyone stands in a circle, speaking each line carefully, and paying attention to each of the sounds in the words. Try it a couple of times, the first time stressing the consonants; the second, exaggerating all the vowel sounds. Then work with both in order to fully articulate the text. Try and put a bit of bounce into the tongue-twister, finding the rhythm and the dance-like nature of the words. Slashes indicate where the beat falls.

> Trini – / dada,
> And the / warm Missi – / ssippi
> And the / town Hono – / lulu
> And the / lake Titti – / cacca.
> The / Poppaki – / tapital is / not in / Canada,
> Rather in / Mexico, / Mexico, / Mexico.
> / Canada, / Malaga, / Rimini, / Brindisi.
> / Canada, / Malaga, / Rimini, / Brindisi.
> / Yes! Ti – / beta, Ti – / beta, Ti – / beta,
> Oh / Yes! Ti – / beta, Ti – / beta, Ti – / beta, oh /
>   yes.

Repeat from the beginning, a bit faster this time.

You can add any gestures and choreography to make this rhyme your own. You could also make up your own geographical tongue-twisters.

The Aim of the Game

This exercise warms up the voice and focuses the group on their articulation before performance.

Players	Skills
Any number	*Voice Work, Projection, Breath Control, Focus, Articulation*

Ensemble

A focus exercise in which the group have to perform an action simultaneously.

How to Play

Everyone stands silently in a circle with their feet hip-width apart and their hands out front, ready to clap. Players should focus on the area in the centre of the circle, rather than looking around or making eye contact with any of the other players.

Without discussion, the group must now attempt to clap simultaneously, so there is just one clap. The idea is that the group will be aware of each other to the extent that they can clap exactly in unison, without anticipating it or watching other players' hands move inwards.

It sounds extremely simple, but it does take a surprising degree of concentration, and often many attempts, before a totally simultaneous sound can be achieved. If the group is struggling, you can always try an easier group reaction first; for example, dropping the head.

The Aim of the Game

This exercise encourages the group to be aware of each other and to work as an ensemble. I often use this as the final exercise of a warm-up with actors before a first performance; it helps to bond the company whilst also focusing them physically and mentally.

Players	Skills
6+	*Ensemble Work, Focus, Control*

INDEX OF GAMES

SKILLS

NUMBERS REFER TO GAMES NOT PAGES

ALPHABETICAL LIST